New Directions for
Student Services

John H. Schuh
EDITOR-IN-CHIEF

Elizabeth J. Whitt
ASSOCIATE EDITOR

D1232615

Case Studies for Implementing Assessment in Student Affairs

Marilee J. Bresciani
Megan Moore Gardner
Jessica Hickmott
EDITORS

Number 127 • Fall 2009
Jossey-Bass
San Francisco

CASE STUDIES FOR IMPLEMENTING ASSESSMENT IN STUDENT AFFAIRS
Marilee J. Bresciani, Megan Moore Gardner, Jessica Hickmott (eds.)
New Directions for Student Services, no. 127
John H. Schuh, Editor-in-Chief
Elizabeth J. Whitt, Associate Editor

NEW DIRECTIONS FOR STUDENT SERVICES (ISSN 0164-7970, e-ISSN 1536-0695) is part of The Jossey-Bass Higher and Adult Education Series and is published quarterly by Wiley Subscription Services, Inc., A Wiley Company, at Jossey-Bass, 989 Market Street, San Francisco, California 94103-1741. Periodicals Postage Paid at San Francisco, California, and at additional mailing offices. POSTMASTER: Send address changes to New Directions for Student Services, Jossey-Bass, 989 Market Street, San Francisco, CA 94103-1741.

New Directions for Student Services is indexed in CIJE: Current Index to Journals in Education (ERIC), Contents Pages in Education (T&F), Current Abstracts (EBSCO), Education Index/Abstracts (H.W. Wilson), Educational Research Abstracts Online (T&F), ERIC Database (Education Resources Information Center), and Higher Education Abstracts (Claremont Graduate University).

Microfilm copies of issues and articles are available in 16mm and 35mm, as well as microfiche in 105mm, through University Microfilms Inc., 300 North Zeeb Road, Ann Arbor, Michigan 48106-1346.

SUBSCRIPTIONS cost $98 for individuals and $267 for institutions, agencies, and libraries in the United States.

EDITORIAL CORRESPONDENCE should be sent to the Editor-in-Chief, John H. Schuh, N 243 Lagomarcino Hall, Iowa State University, Ames, Iowa 50011.

www.josseybass.com

CONTENTS

EDITORS' NOTES

The purpose of this issue of *New Directions for Student Services* is to present case studies of assessment in student affairs and student services in a manner that allows the reader to understand the institutional context for the case(s) on which the reader is reflecting. These case studies are intended to assist faculty and administrators in reflective implementation of student learning and development within their division of student affairs. In addition, the case studies will assist readers in garnering information about what was learned from evaluating student development and learning, and what may be avoided in the future.

The art of reflection, as Dewey (1933) and Schön (1983) describe it, is a very rich process for evaluating concepts and ideas. Often, in our desire to implement something that seems mandated, the art of reflection goes completely out the window and we are left with how-to books and checklists, pigeonholing what we do into a "good-practice" model and calling it good. How-to books, checklists, and good-practice models all have their value and are most certainly helpful. However, when one does not have time for reflection, the use of these resources may actually hinder implementation of reflective practice that is sustainable. Without the ability to consider just why and how these models may be of value at our institutions, we run the risk of meeting a deadline but risking the long-term investment in reflective practice, and thus risking implementation of outcomes-based assessment that is sustainable. Given that assessment is intended to create reflective systematic inquiry processes, it seems almost ironic that those practices are often implemented without meaningful reflection.

It is hoped that, while you are reflectively reviewing these various case studies, you will notice that there are several ways in which to evaluate student learning and development within student affairs. Each case varies in its approach, and each contributing author shares tips for implementing assessment as well as challenges.

This issue is not a how-to on engaging in assessment of student learning and development. The Bresciani, Moore Gardner, and Hickmott (2009) book, titled *Demonstrating Student Success in Student Affairs,* is designed as a how-to, and much of the research that informed the contents of that book was drawn from many of these case studies. This issue of *New Directions for Student Services* is designed to give practical advice through examples for consideration when implementing assessment of student learning and development on your own campus. In essence, this issue supplements *Demonstrating Student Success in Student Affairs* and is filled with detailed examples.

NEW DIRECTIONS FOR STUDENT SERVICES, no. 127, Fall 2009 © Wiley Periodicals, Inc.
Published online in Wiley InterScience (www.interscience.wiley.com) • DOI: 10.1002/ss.321

1

Following the brief description of what is contained in each case study and an explanation of how the cases were selected, questions to guide you through each study are proposed. Such questions are intended to further aid the reflective evaluation of each case.

Selection of Case Studies

An open invitation for submission of a case study, based on specific criteria, was made to all institutions that belong to the National Association of Student Personnel Administrators (NASPA) via an avenue approved by the NASPA office. In addition, the editors examined institutional websites and explored conference proceedings to invite additional participants' submissions. The compilation of case studies included in this issue represents a mixture of good practices for outcomes-based assessment and illustrations of other types of assessment. The richness of examples is intended to offer you myriad illustrations, as well as advise you on challenges that are often faced by those implementing assessment within student affairs.

Contents of Each Case Study/Chapter. Each case study serves as its own chapter. Included in each case for your benefit are:

1. Overview of institutional culture
2. Overview of the division of student affairs/services
3. Overview of assessment process within the division of student affairs/services
4. Examples of assessment and how results are used
5. Tips for implementing process
6. Description of barrier to assessing student learning and development, and an illustration of the strategy to overcome it
7. References

Suggested Considerations and Questions When Reflecting on Each Case. These case studies are designed to be used in graduate preparation programs to complement the *Demonstrating Student Success in Student Affairs* book. Or they may be used by professionals to stimulate ideas as they implement practices on their own campus. Regardless of how you choose to use these case studies, keep in mind that they were written at a certain point in time and therefore you may safely assume that the practice of the institutions represented has most likely changed since publication of this issue. The contributing authors' names and institutions are included with each case so that you may contact them for updates or further ideas on their work with assessment.

Questions to Consider for Each Case

As you proceed through each case, whether you work in groups or on your own, consider these reflective questions.

1. How has the institution conceptualized assessment? If you desire more assistance in understanding the various types of assessment and the reasons to use each type, see *Demonstrating Student Success in Student Affairs*, Chapters 1 and 2. Understanding how each institution has conceptualized assessment aids you in knowing whether their example will be of further benefit to you. If you are unsure how your institution conceptualizes assessment, see "Outcomes-Based Academic and Co-Curricular Program Review: A Compilation of Institutional Good Practices" (Chapter 5 in that volume) for a list of questions to consider in regard to formulating your institutional conceptual framework for assessment.

2. What at the institution or within that division of student affairs/services is similar to your own in regard to institutional type, culture, and perceptions of, and collaborations with, student affairs/services? Examining similarities and differences in the institutions from which you are borrowing good ideas can help you note rather quickly what may work and why, thus saving you valuable time.

3. What are similarities in your assessment processes with the institutions in the case studies? Would you make any modifications to your process, on the basis of what you are reading?

4. Where there are no similarities, what would you like to adopt in practice? Why? How would it fit in with your institutional and divisional culture?

5. How well does their process seem to deliver the types of results they expect?

6. How well does their process seem to sustain the purpose of their division? their institutional culture?

7. How meaningful to the leaders at your institution is the manner in which they used the results?

8. How well do their results seem to sustain their systematic assessment process? the purpose of their division? their institutional culture?

9. How many of the helpful tips can be incorporated into your practice, given your institutional and divisional culture?

10. Overall, what do you specifically admire about their practice? Why?

11. What would you change about their practice? Why?

12. What resources can be of value to you and your colleagues? in what context? Specifically, how would you use those resources?

13. When reviewing the barriers section, consider these additional questions, which were adapted from Ashbaugh and Kasten (1995):

- Identify the central barrier posed.
- Identify a secondary barrier posed. Locate evidence to support identification of the central problem and the secondary problems.
- Develop alternative solutions through brainstorming, *or*
- Evaluate the alternatives proposed (if they are present).

- If they are present, select the alternative most likely to solve the problem or bring about the desired change at your institution; or suggest a new solution.
- Discuss how you would implement the solution.

14. If the case study illustrates an outcomes-based assessment practice, how well does the practice meet criteria illustrated in documents published by AAHE (1992); Bresciani (2006); Bresciani, Moore Gardner, and Hickmott (2009); Kuh, Kinzie, Schuh, and Whitt (2005); Maki (2004); Palomba and Banta (1999); and Suskie (2004)?

Summary

This issue is truly intended to promote reflection about what constitutes good practice in implementing assessment within student affairs/services at your institution. It is not anticipated that you will adopt the practices introduced in each of these case studies without consideration of the aforementioned questions. Rather, it is our intent in compiling these examples that you review them with a critical eye, glean from them what is meaningful to you and your institution, and learn from the lessons the contributing authors so richly and generously share.

Acknowledgments

This issue of *New Directions for Student Services* is dedicated to those who have worked so diligently to improve student learning and development in the co-curricular. We applaud you—you whose work has been published and presented to others in an effort to help others improve, and to those whose work has not yet been published or yet recognized. To all of you, thank you for being intentional about planning and implementing your practice. Thank you for allocating time to reflectively improve that practice. Thank you for demonstrating the care and concern you have for student success. Thank you for helping to build a body of evidence on how the co-curricular contributes to student learning and development. Thank you for the knowledge, wisdom, and challenging questions you have shared and will continue to share with us all.

In addition, we thank all of our friends, family members, and colleagues who supported us in the compilation of this resource. It truly "takes a village" to raise what we hope will come to be a thought-provoking resource.

References

American Association of Higher Education (AAHE). "Nine Principles of Good Practice for Assessing Student Learning." 1992. Retrieved Mar. 16, 2006, from http://www.academicprograms.calpoly.edu/pdfs/assess/nine_principles_good_practice.pdf.

Ashbaugh, C. R., and Kasten, K. L. *Educational Leadership: Case Studies.* London: Long-man, 1995.

Bresciani, M. J. *Outcomes-Based Academic and Co-Curricular Program Review: A Compilation of Institutional Good Practices.* Sterling, Va.: Stylus, 2006.

Bresciani, M. J., Moore Gardner, M., and Hickmott, J. *Demonstrating Student Success in Student Affairs.* Sterling, Va.: Stylus, 2009.

Dewey, J. *How We Think: A Restatement of the Relation of Reflective Thinking to the Educative Process.* Boston: Heath, 1933.

Kuh, G. D., Kinzie, J., Schuh, J. H., and Whitt, E. J. *Assessing Conditions to Enhance Educational Effectiveness.* San Francisco: Jossey-Bass, 2005.

Maki, P. *Assessing for Student Learning: Building a Sustainable Commitment Across the Institution.* Sterling, Va.: Stylus, 2004.

Palomba, C., and Banta, T. *Assessment Essentials: Planning, Implementing, and Improving Assessment in Higher Education.* San Francisco: Jossey-Bass, 1999.

Schön, D. A. *How Professionals Think in Action.* New York: Basic Books, 1983.

Suskie, L. *Assessing Student Learning: A Common Sense Guide.* Bolton, Mass.: Anker, 2004.

MARILEE J. BRESCIANI *is a professor of postsecondary education and codirector of the Center for Educational Leadership, Innovation, and Policy at San Diego State University.*

MEGAN MOORE GARDNER *is an assistant professor of higher education administration at the University of Akron.*

JESSICA HICKMOTT *is the student affairs assessment coordinator at Weber State University.*

NEW DIRECTIONS FOR STUDENT SERVICES • DOI: 10.1002/ss

1

This chapter provides a glimpse of student affairs assessment at Alverno College including a specific example of assessment, tips to implementing assessment at your institution, and barriers encountered when implementing the process at Alverno College.

Alverno College

Virginia Wagner

Overview of Institutional Culture

Alverno College is a private, liberal arts college located in a residential neighborhood on the southwest side of Milwaukee, Wisconsin. In fall 2008, the student body numbered 2,783, and there were 231 resident students. The student body is highly diverse (34 percent minority), and most students commute to campus for their classes. The culture at Alverno is distinguished by a focus on student learning, a commitment to quality improvement, and collaboration.

What distinguishes Alverno from most other colleges is its ability-based curriculum and assessment process, a unique approach to teaching and learning that was initiated in 1973. Alverno is known for its ability-based curriculum, its use of performance assessment across the curriculum, and its focus on self-assessment. The distinctive feature of the ability-based approach is that faculty make explicit the expectation that *students should be able to do something with what they know.* Many of you have probably asked, "What do students learn as a result of participating in the co-curriculum, and how is this learning different from the classroom?" This was our question several years ago as we began a process of articulating the importance of learning in the co-curriculum. Now we ask students the question.

Overview of Division of Student Affairs/Services

The Division of Student Services is composed of five departments: Campus Ministry, Counseling and Health Services, Office of Student Services,

NEW DIRECTIONS FOR STUDENT SERVICES, no. 127, Fall 2009 © Wiley Periodicals, Inc.
Published online in Wiley InterScience (www.interscience.wiley.com) • DOI: 10.1002/ss.322

Residence Life, and Student Services. Our mission is to "partner with others in building community." We consider students, faculty, staff, parents, and the Milwaukee community our partners as we engage students in learning experiences and create a dynamic learning environment. A CA (community advisor) aptly described her integrated learning experience: "I know that Alverno is all about bringing learning to life, but there is no way that a classroom experience can compare to 'living in and with' what I am learning. Living in the residence halls has been my social and cultural education."

In 1995, the Student Services staff began discussions about how to intentionally extend the learning environment beyond the classroom and integrate the teaching and learning principles into the co-curriculum. We met with faculty to gain insights and focused on three questions to better understand our role in student learning:

1. What is worth teaching in the co-curriculum? If co-curricular activities and staff were eliminated on campus, what learning would not happen?
2. What changes in the Alverno culture need to be made to address the co-curriculum? Are there assumptions that need to be challenged? (E.g., students are too busy to be involved because they need to work long hours to afford college. Nontraditional students do not have the time or interest in being involved.)
3. Are we explicit about our expectations? Do students know what is expected in the residence hall? on the court? in the cafeteria? in the classroom? off campus?

Our questions and discussions helped us create a vision to collaborate with students, faculty, and staff to create a shared view and experience of learning where the curriculum and co-curriculum work together to promote the personal and professional development of students.

Overview of the Assessment Process

Throughout the years, Alverno hosted workshops for educators to learn about the ability-based curriculum. Educators often asked staff how they use the abilities in their work with students. This prompted a group of staff from various departments (Academic Services, Admissions, Advising, Alumnae, Human Resources, Student Life, and Student Services) to meet and discuss how we are integral to the teaching and learning process. The goals of the group were to:

• Explain the relationship between the curriculum and the learning environment.
• Articulate the importance of our work to the educational process.
• Describe the Alverno culture and identify future needs.

- Identify roles and components of the culture and the relationship to the curriculum.
- Incorporate what we learn so that we articulate it internally and externally and thereby continuously improve our practice.

Over the course of the discussions, the staff produced a paper titled "Partners in Learning: Staff Collaboration in Promoting Student Learning Across the College." This paper is introduced to and discussed with all new employees during their orientation to the college. They learn about the importance of their role in creating a positive learning environment and assisting students to be successful.

As the Student Services Staff developed learning outcomes for the co-curriculum, it became clear that this process was time-consuming. Staff sometimes wondered why we were adding another level of work to our responsibilities. After some discussion, we came up with a number of reasons developing learning outcomes was helpful:

- Positions Student Services in the college as co-educators
- Makes teaching and learning public and explicit
- Clarifies the role of the department and sets a focus
- Integrates skills, knowledge, attitudes, and dispositions
- Imparts direction for learning in our area of responsibility
- Gives us more control over what is evaluated
- Provides more continuity and consistency
- Assists us to improve practice with evidence and come to know what we are and are not improving
- Promotes balance between focusing on the student and meeting the expectations of the college

Tips for Implementing the Process

After you read this, you may have some questions. "Where do we start? Can we really do this on our campus? What fits best with the educational philosophy on our campus?" This was our process on our campus:

Step one: Link department mission to the college mission.
Step two: Align structures to serve student learning.
Step three: Articulate assumptions about the relationship between the curriculum and the co-curriculum.
Step four: Find frameworks(s) that work. We are very fortunate because we build on and use Alverno's educational philosophy. The frameworks we use are from the curriculum. We use the ability-based education, the performance-based approach, the abilities, and student assessment as learning. What this means for us is that we focus on individual student learning based on:

- Explicit student learning outcomes and explicit criteria
- Student performance
- Observation, analysis, interpretation, and judgment of each student's performance
- Student self-assessment and feedback to students

Step five: Develop outcomes (department, program, and individual student) that are linked to the college's learning outcomes. The abilities used within the curriculum are:

1. Communication
2. Analysis
3. Problem solving
4. Valuing in decision making
5. Social interaction
6. Developing a global perspective
7. Effective citizenship
8. Aesthetic engagement

We believe that some of the abilities relate more directly to our work in Student Services. We chose to focus on four abilities:

In *social interaction,* students practice working effectively with others in a variety of situations.
In *problem solving,* students analyze and solve problems.
In *effective citizenship,* students are leaders, involved and responsible to their community.
In *valuing,* students learn to appreciate others' values and apply their values to concrete situations.

We developed individual student learning outcomes for the students we directly influence and use teachable moments as we work with all students to remind them to draw on the abilities learned in the curriculum (as an example, in residence life when conflicts emerge; student group conflict). The process includes a session with the students at the beginning of the semester to talk about the learning outcomes and expectations. Then following the sport season or at the end of the semester, the student completes a self-assessment. She then sits down with the coach or supervisor to receive oral and written feedback and determine goals to improve her performance. Here are some examples of the learning outcomes we have developed:

Athletics	Shows respect for self and other players
	Shows enthusiasm and promotes good team spirit and morale
	Identifies team goals and works toward achieving them
	Uses social interaction skills to offer positive reinforcement and appreciation for others

Campus ministry	Accurately identifies the audience and is inclusive of all people regardless of their faith tradition
	Demonstrates openness to feedback to improve skills
	Takes initiative in suggesting new programming ideas
Residence life CA (community advisor) staff	Involves others in planning events
	Works directly with residents to mediate and resolve conflicts and disagreements consistently and respectfully
	Accepts and uses team feedback
Student Life Programming Board	Assesses student needs and uses the information to offer programs to meet the diverse needs of students
	Involves volunteers in planning events
	Asks questions when unsure of something
	Communicates concerns, frustrations, suggestions, and feedback appropriately
Student worker staff	Seeks further training or help when needed
	Takes responsibility for timely completion of duties, tasks, and projects
	Treats customers with respect and friendliness

We also developed criteria for activities and programs offered. The CA (community advisors) staff and students involved in programming use these criteria to evaluate their programs:

Activity and program evaluation for the students planning programs	Meets the goals for the event
	Provides opportunities for students to extend abilities into their personal and professional lives
	Involves effective collaboration
	Promotes successful student involvement in creating co-curricular activities
	Responds effectively to needs or critical issues of the Alverno community, using the Wellness Model as a resource
	Creates a variety of interactive and individual opportunities (passive programming) designed to have impact on a diverse student population
	Elicits positive response from participants
	Involves enough participants to make it worth offering
	Identifies the primary audience and plans with sensitivity (e.g., faith traditions, cultures, ages, issues)

Step six: Determine evaluation and assessment methods.

Overcoming Barriers to Assessing Student Learning and Development

We face several challenges in assessing student learning. One is the ongoing training of new staff and helping them understand the culture of Alverno and Student Services. This involves educating staff about learning outcomes and valuing the importance of self-assessment and feedback. Training staff to understand Alverno's philosophy of education and how it is integrated in the co-curriculum can be challenging. One of the best ways we have found to integrate staff is to involve them in the curriculum so that they have an understanding and foundation. We do this by asking them to be trained as out-of-class assessors in social interaction.

Most colleges focus on program assessment. We focus on individual student assessment as well. Another challenge we face is writing clear outcomes that make sense to us and to the students. This is a challenge that many of you may also experience. We consult with individuals who are great resources to us such as local and national assessment experts and students who provide useful feedback as we develop and write student learning outcomes.

VIRGINIA WAGNER *is the associate vice president for student services at Alverno College.*

NEW DIRECTIONS FOR STUDENT SERVICES • DOI: 10.1002/ss

2

This chapter provides a glimpse of student affairs assessment at Colorado State University including a specific example of assessment, tips to implementing assessment at your institution, and barriers encountered when implementing the process at Colorado State University.

Colorado State University

David A. McKelfresh, Kim K. Bender

Overview of Institutional Culture

Colorado State University is located in Fort Collins, which is a midsize city of 134,000 situated in Northern Colorado at the western edge of the Great Plains and at the base of the Rocky Mountains. CSU's total enrollment is approximately twenty-five thousand students.

The Division of Student Affairs comprises thirty departments organized into programmatic clusters: Advocacy Programs, Academic Support Services, Campus Life, Housing and Dining Services, Lory Student Center, Parent and Family Programs, and Wellness Programs and Services. The vice president for student affairs reports to the senior vice president/provost, who reports to the president.

Overview of the Division of Student Affairs/Services

The division offers a variety of programs and services designed to help students succeed and grow. The effectiveness and improvement of these programs and services are detailed under Student Affairs Strategic Goals related to "Teaching and Learning" (http://www.president.colostate.edu/strategic-planning/index.asp?page=sd_march06_learning):

1. A diverse community
2. Assessment
3. Experiential learning and other co-curricular opportunities

NEW DIRECTIONS FOR STUDENT SERVICES, no. 127, Fall 2009   © Wiley Periodicals, Inc.
Published online in Wiley InterScience (www.interscience.wiley.com) • DOI: 10.1002/ss.323

4. Student access and retention
5. Student health and safety
6. Quality student affairs staffing
7. Quality venues and related services that support learning
8. Partnerships

Vision statement: A Colorado State University campus environment that fully engages students in the development of their unique potential.

Mission statement: The Division of Student Affairs provides services and programs integral to the academic mission of the university that prepare students to:

- Maximize their collegiate experience
- Integrate academic and personal development
- Assume self- and social responsibility
- Value well-being in body, mind, spirit, and community
- Embrace an ongoing passion for discovery, inquiry, and critical thinking
- Appreciate and respect diverse peoples, ideas, talents, abilities, and cultures
- Establish lasting connections with Colorado State University and its traditions
- Contribute in positive and productive ways to their personal and professional communities
- Become environmentally and globally aware citizens

Overview of the Assessment Process

Planning and evaluating for student development using PRISM. Colorado State University operates a campuswide continuous improvement system known as PRISM, or Plan for Researching Improvement and Supporting Mission. Nearly all CSU academic programs, undergraduate and graduate (169), and student affairs units (28) have developed assessment plans in the PRISM online database. Maintaining both academic and student affairs assessment plans in the same university database symbolizes the emphasis the university places on collaboration between student affairs and academic programs to affect student learning and character development.

The interactive webpage environment gives student affairs programs a place for staff to (1) articulate their values about quality, (2) create student development outcomes, (3) view the strategies that units use to have students achieve their development goals, (4) explore the assessment or research methods that programs use to determine progress, and (5) learn of the improvements being implemented to strengthen student performance.

There are ten components of the system; the critical components for the Division of Student Affairs are described in the paragraphs that follow.

Critical Parts of the System

Component five: Planning integration. Assessment of student learning and development outcomes is unlikely to be sustainable within student affairs units at larger decentralized universities if staff members continue to view this effort as a low-stakes activity that is isolated from a unit's work plan, annual reporting process, program review, or the institutional strategic plan. Therefore, the Division of Student Affairs is working toward linking all of these planning activities in a common university database. The online assessment plans that now exist are to become embedded automatically within program review self-studies, thereby adding visibility and account-ability for those units doing annual assessment of student development out-comes and for those that do not. The database format enables units to electronically link their program review action plan goals directly with metrics of the institutional strategic plan, showing which areas of strategic planning attract the most or the least planning activity. Easy access to insti-tutionwide student satisfaction survey results, student course survey results, and unit-based surveys uploaded from Student Voice survey services further informs planning and evaluation efforts. The database integration of plan-ning will permit the student development findings and resulting improve-ments to migrate automatically from assessment plans to units' annual reports. This integration makes the research of student development out-comes a higher-stakes activity, giving leverage to the university enterprise of preparing its students to graduate with those developmental attributes valued by the campus community.

Component six: Peer review and organizational learning environments. Like many institutions, the student affairs division uses a steering commit-tee to guide assessment efforts for student development outcomes and annu-ally review student affairs assessment plans. Using a common rubric of planning and evaluation standards of best practice, these committee mem-bers embed online comments into assessment plans to improve outcome descriptions and evaluation methods. The peer review subcommittees involve graduate students from the student affairs master's program to gain their perspective and to advance their development for the workplace.

Additionally, student affairs staff members use PRISM's online orga-nizational learning environment as a place to learn about one another's planning and evaluation activities, especially those related to student development outcomes. Change and improvement are accelerated when staff members go online to view planning outcomes and explore units' best practices, within and across divisions. Performance research evaluation instruments, such as rubrics or interview forms, are uploaded into plan-ning outcomes and are shared campuswide. Those assessment plans that use collaborative methods among academic and student affairs depart-ments are highlighted to encourage more of this cooperation. By fostering applied learning opportunities for students of academic departments, student affairs units help determine the effectiveness of students' academic preparation. This symbiotic relationship is articulated in assessment plans.

Using their standards rubric, peer-review groups actively guide or direct planning design so that it (1) generates evidence needed by regional accreditation bodies, (2) strengthens compliance with professional association standards, (3) supports the institution's strategic planning metrics, or (4) meets state accountability expectations. Peer review of planning has become an excellent method for implementing the university's strategic plan. In addition, members ensure that program plans are discovering performance strengths and weaknesses, not just confirming or monitoring activity levels. The experience serves as leadership training for rising staff members, because committee members become experts in the best practices of departmental planning, self-evaluation, organizational management, and systematic improvement. Knowledge of effective unit or department organizational strategies for improving learning, research, and service are systematically distributed to different staff every year as peer-review membership changes and program review committees rotate staff members.

Examples of Assessment and How Results Are Used

Apartment Life. Housing and Dining Services mission statement: Provide clean, safe, well-maintained, attractive, and reasonably priced living environments for students and customers, which are supportive of the educational mission of the university. Offer nutritious and desirable food with the highest standard of service in a pleasant and attractive environment. To support the intellectual, physical, social, emotional, and spiritual development of on-campus residents. Apartment Life mission statement: Apartment Life creates a living-learning community founded on the strength of our differences, interests, and common goals. Our vision is to impact each member of the Apartment Life community, fostering interaction, understanding, and appreciation among people of all backgrounds. Through this positive experience with our residents, we can ultimately influence the university, Fort Collins, and the world.

Assessment process. The assessment activities of Apartment Life are driven by the organization's mission and strategic goals, and the Office of Housing and Dining Service's vision, mission, and strategic goals. Apartment Life has measurable evaluation criteria. Quantitative and qualitative data are collected from multiple sources. The H&DS director of assessment coordinates the assessment process with input from all of the H&DS directors staff. The director of assessment meets weekly with the director of H&DS to review assessment activities. Assessment reports are furnished to internal and external constituencies. Assessment information informs departmental strategic planning and programmatic improvement. A full review of all H&DS assessments can be seen in the Division of Student Affairs assessment database,

NEW DIRECTIONS FOR STUDENT SERVICES • DOI: 10.1002/ss

which is located on the Division of Student Affairs website on the Assessment and Research Steering Committee weblink.

Here are specific examples of Apartment Life outcomes, evaluation methods, criteria, and decisions based on results:

- *Outcomes.* Apartment residents will have a positive response to their overall Apartment Life experience regarding:

  Experience: Overall satisfaction with apartment living experience.
  Expectations: To what extent did the apartment experience fulfill student expectations?
  Overall value: Comparing cost to quality, rate the overall value of the apartment experience.

- Apartment residents will have a positive response to opportunities for intercultural interaction and appreciation of cultural differences related to:

  Satisfaction with cultural activities
  Fellow residents and their level of satisfaction regarding their respect for differences
  Fellow residents and their respect for differences of gender

- Apartment residents will have a positive experience with regard to their personal growth while living in the apartments, specifically the extent to which living in an apartment enhances your ability to:

  Meet people
  Study more effectively
  Manage your time more effectively
  Adopt a healthy lifestyle
  Appreciate different cultures

- Apartment residents will have a positive experience with regard to the ability to achieve their academic goals and the extent to which living in an apartment enhances the ability to study more effectively.

Assessment methods. Two primary assessments are used:

- Apartment Life Exit Survey: The Apartment Life Exit Survey is given to residents as they begin the "vacate" process from their apartment. Results are tabulated twice every year, once at the end of fall semester and once in the summer.
- Annual EBI Apartment Satisfaction Survey: The EBI Apartment Survey is administered as an electronic survey each year by the Apartment Life staff in the spring to 100 percent of the resident population. The overall return rate is above 65 percent. The EBI assessment supplies each department with a Self-Assessment, a Comparative Assessment (to compare to similar

departments at similar institutions), and Continuous Assessment (a comparison of longitudinal trends).

Decisions based on results:

- Developed three separate new student orientations for Saudi students, first-year undergraduate students, and all other undergraduate students living in the ICC.
- Collaborated with the Office of Admissions and the Office of International Programs on development and implementation of Global Nomads orientation program.
- Successfully expanded the Intercultural Connections Program to more than 185 participants and anticipate[d] enrollment of more than 200 students for fall 2007, which includes specific recruitment activities from the Study Abroad Fair, Housing Fair, transfer student orientation, international student orientations, and advocacy offices.

Tips for Implementing the Process

Replication or adoption of the following is encouraged:

- Designate one staff member in the Division of Student Affairs to coordinate and give direction to divisionwide assessment efforts. Preferably this position would focus full-time efforts toward assessment.
- Clear direction and support from the president and VP for student affairs
- Implement an Assessment Steering Committee to guide divisionwide assessment strategy and initiatives. Membership on the committee preferably would represent all functional areas of the division.
- Develop partnerships with the staff members in other parts of the university who are responsible for assessment and research (e.g., Provost's Office, Institutional Research).
- Conduct an audit of all assessments done by each department in the division.

This general advice is offered:

- Establish regular training sessions and individual coaching support for staff members in each department.
- Provide ongoing communication regarding assessment results and how departments are using assessment.
- Make available online resources for staff members conducting assessment.
- Be patient and methodical; it takes approximately four or five years to develop your assessment program.
- Make assessment a part of the divisional strategic plan, a part of each department's annual goal and objectives, a part of the each department's annual report, and a part of the division annual report.

NEW DIRECTIONS FOR STUDENT SERVICES • DOI: 10.1002/ss

Overcoming Barriers to Assessing Student Learning and Development

Although colleges and universities have been evaluating themselves for decades, the old processes for assessment, program review, and strategic planning still suffer from structural negative factors, such as administrative turnover, episodic self-evaluation, disjunctive planning efforts, department isolation, and the schism often separating the academic and student affairs communities. These factors frustrate the public's concern for accountability, retard the cycles of institutional improvement, and reinforce what Joseph Burke (2007) calls "the fragmented university."

The PRISM process records planning and evaluation activity over time. This avoids reliance on one or two influential administrators who might leave the institution. The database timelines require a regular reporting sequence that tends to establish assessment activity as a ritual over time. Integration of annual assessment, five-year program review, and strategic planning connects the multiple levels of planning and reveals aggregations of effort for more effective resource allocation. The structural collaborative assessment planning among academic and student affairs units also mitigates the intensity of a fragmented organization. The information transparency that the system provides for university constituents reduces the insular state of some student affairs units, giving their assessment information more impact with a wider audience.

Additionally, Colorado State University has become one of the first universities to join a national effort by participating in College Portrait, a pilot transparency program of the National Association of State Universities and Land Grant Colleges (NASULGC). The university duplicates its College Portrait on its own admissions webpage: http://wsprod.colostate.edu/cwis43/admissions/ccs/VSA.pdf.

References

Burke, J. C. *Fixing the Fragmented University: Decentralization with Direction.* Bolton, Mass.: Anker, 2007.

CSU Strategic Goals 2006–2009. "Setting the Standard for the 21st Century University Teaching." n.d. Retrieved June 6, 2007, from http://www.president.colostate.edu/strategicplanning/index.asp?page=sd_march06_learning.

DAVID A. MCKELFRESH *currently serves on a joint appoint at Colorado State University as the executive director of assessment and research for the Division of Student Affairs, and as program chair for the Student Affairs in Higher Education graduate program.*

KIM K. BENDER *is the director of assessment at Colorado State University.*

NEW DIRECTIONS FOR STUDENT SERVICES • DOI: 10.1002/ss

3

This chapter provides a glimpse of student affairs assessment at Frederick Community College including a specific example of assessment, tips to implementing assessment at your institution, and barriers encountered when implementing the process at Frederick Community College.

Frederick Community College

L. Richard Haney, Debralee McClellan

Overview of Institutional Culture

Frederick Community College (FCC) is a comprehensive open-door community college that serves the citizens of Frederick County, Maryland, the state's largest county by size and seventh in population (230,000). It is located in central Maryland, equidistant from Baltimore and Washington, D.C. It is the college of choice for Frederick County; two-thirds of county residents who are enrolled in undergraduate programs are enrolled at FCC. The average student age is twenty-seven, 61.5 percent attend part-time, and 63 percent are female. Students of color make up 18.9 percent of the student population. Approximately 61 percent of students are enrolled in transfer programs, a longstanding trend at the college. The college's character as a learning college is represented by its vision statement, "Student Learning First." In 2002, FCC carried out a campuswide visioning day that launched its transition to a "learning college" organizational model. The learning college concept places learning at the center of the institution and makes the college responsible for student learning (O'Banion, 1997). The college's reorganization as a learning college resulted in a nontraditional structure with three main organizational areas: Learning, Learning Support, and Administration, each led by a vice president. The Student Development Division was renamed Learning Support to emphasize its role in supporting student learning. As part of the reorganization, several functions were realigned or consolidated, and one major new function, Information Technology, was added.

NEW DIRECTIONS FOR STUDENT SERVICES, no. 127, Fall 2009   © Wiley Periodicals, Inc.
Published online in Wiley InterScience (www.interscience.wiley.com) • DOI: 10.1002/ss.324

Overview of Division of Student Affairs/Services

The need for student affairs professionals "to participate in institution-wide efforts to assess student learning" (American College Personnel Association [ACPA], 1996, p. 5) and "use systematic inquiry to improve student and institutional performance" (ACPA and National Association of Student Personnel Administrators [NASPA], 1997, p. 1) was emphasized in the mid-1990s. Student affairs professionals were asked not just to participate but also to lead broad efforts to assess student learning as a means to participate more fully in the learning enterprise (ACPA and NASPA, 2004). The need for FCC's student affairs staff to be engaged in assessment of student learning was clear because research indicated that learning occurs outside the classroom as well as inside the classroom.

Learning Support comprises the Offices of Enrollment Management, Student Development (Advising and Counseling, Services for Students with Disabilities, Multicultural Student Support Services, Career Services, and Adult Services), Financial Aid, Student Life, Intercollegiate Athletics, and Information Technology. A director or associate vice president manages each department, and strong communication exists within the Learning Support division.

With the college's reorganization into a learning college, a new mission statement that reflected the learning college philosophy was developed at a staff retreat in 2004. It states: "Learning Support provides services in a changing professional environment that encourages and supports learning and goal attainment."

According to the college's vice president for learning, faculty and administrator expectations of student services depend on what functions are in student services. In general, they want to see students who are well advised, engaged with the college, and retained from one semester to the next so that they complete their programs or transfer within a reasonable period of time. They also want to see support for curricular initiatives (for example, student life's minigrant program for co-curricular program development) and support for their work with students within and outside the classroom (classroom behavior, troubled students, and so on).

Overview of the Assessment Process

Assessment of student services at the college has, for a long time, focused on traditional institutional effectiveness measures and student satisfaction. The transition to a learning college moved beyond use of student satisfaction measures to using measures of student learning and development (Bresciani, 2002). How the college made this transition is discussed later in the case study.

The Learning Support division provides a variety of programs and services that engage students in the process of academic and personal development. All Learning Support programs contribute to the learning outcome that students will become self-directed learners. That is, students will develop the ability to establish educational and career goals, devise an educational plan to meet established goals, and demonstrate awareness of college policies, procedures, and resources and services.

Additionally, through their involvement with Learning Support programming, students develop leadership and learning management skills to enable them to achieve academic success. They will also demonstrate civic engagement and service skills needed for their participation as engaged members of their community. In terms of personal growth and development, students are expected to attain a realistic appreciation of self and others, demonstrate respect for individual differences, gain self-confidence, identify individual strengths and abilities, and clarify personal values.

In developing assessment plans every year, Learning Support units now develop, where appropriate, "learning-based" indicators. Although all learning support areas have made progress in this regard, learning-based outcomes are probably best realized in the plans for the Student Development and Student Life departments. Here is an example from Student Life:

Goal/objective: Students will become self-directed learners by developing personal, organizational, and community awareness and will strengthen communication, interpersonal, and critical-thinking and problem-solving skills.

Expected outcomes:

- Student leaders will demonstrate increased self-awareness and enhanced leadership skills in six core competency areas
- Student leaders will assess, examine, and clarify their personal values, beliefs, and goals to better understand their roles as leaders in the college, community, and greater society
- Student leaders will demonstrate a commitment to improving their community through service, programmatic, and personal initiatives
- Student leaders will examine issues from multiple perspectives and be able to conceptualize and apply various approaches to problem solving

Currently, faculty members are informally involved in Learning Support assessment efforts, although, in Student Life's co-curricular programming, they play an active role in development of learning outcomes for the program. To strengthen connections with the faculty, the membership of the college's Outcomes Assessment Council (OAC) was recently broadened to include membership from Learning Support; the associate vice president for student development is a member and now serves as liaison on assessment for the division. OAC, a group of faculty and learning administrators, meet twice every semester to report on and review the progress of learning outcomes included in the college's student learning outcomes assessment plan (SLOAP).

NEW DIRECTIONS FOR STUDENT SERVICES • DOI: 10.1002/ss

The college's planning-assessment-improvement process, begun in 2002, refocused assessment efforts on student learning. This necessitated substantial changes in how assessment of student services was conducted at the college. Assessment of student services was fragmented, lacked specificity, was not well integrated with collegewide assessment efforts, and focused primarily on student satisfaction rather than student learning. To establish the foundation for development of an assessment plan focused on student learning, a multisession divisionwide retreat ("The Learning Imperative: Student Development's Role in the Learning College" and "Outcomes Assessment in the Learning College") was held in 2003.

A confluence of factors led to a major restructuring of assessment efforts in Learning Support and development of a comprehensive assessment plan for the division. By building on these initiatives and adapting concepts from various assessment workshops and activities as well as literature related to assessment, we developed the framework included in our example of assessment below. Assessment plans were finalized by the summer of 2004, and managers submitted their first annual report for the 2004–05 year in July 2005. The reports included a detailed narrative with analysis of the assessment data and a description of how data were used to inform decision making and improve program and services; it also described how the unit's efforts contributed to student learning. By the time of the Middle States accreditation team's visit in March 2006, an assessment system was well under way.

At the beginning of the academic year, a divisionwide meeting is held to review the college's strategic plan, develop annual goals and objectives for the division that link to the strategic plan, and design unit initiatives to accomplish the goals and objectives. The plan is further refined at follow-up meetings with the executive team. Each unit updates its assessment plan by revising or adding additional assessment indicators, modifying expected benchmarks, and updating strategies for the year.

Progress by the units is tracked periodically throughout the year and discussed with the vice president midyear. In addition, the vice president sends quarterly updates to the President's Cabinet on the division's progress on the strategic plan. Results are discussed during the managers' evaluation conference, and changes are made in the plan if needed.

Students are involved both directly and indirectly in the assessment process. Many of the assessment measures that are used involve student rating of criteria identified to measure the expected outcomes. Assessment tools often involve surveys, program evaluations, and other subjective instruments that furnish student feedback on the outcomes being addressed.

Additionally, some Learning Support program assessments, such as Student Life, involve a portfolio evaluation process in which students are actively engaged. Indirect measures of student learning are also used and can include evaluation of student transcripts and measures of academic success and retention that are based on student performance but not reported directly by students.

Example of Assessment and How Results Are Used

One example of learning-based outcomes is reflected in the plan created by the Counseling and Advising Office. The office is responsible for providing academic advising to all new students matriculating into the institution. One of the goals and objectives and the corresponding learning-based outcomes developed by the office as part of its assessment plan are presented in Figure 3.1.

The outcomes are developmental in nature. That is, students will most likely progress toward becoming self-directed learners over a period of time, by way of a series of interventions or strategies made available through the college's academic advising process. An assessment project was undertaken to assess the foundational, or first, intervention given to students—the first-year advising program—the process through which the majority of new students matriculate into the institution.

All students participating in the first-year advising program during the summer of 2006 were asked to complete an evaluation at the conclusion of the program. A total of 734 students participated in the program and 233 responses were received, representing a 32 percent response rate. Students were asked to complete a locally developed survey using a four-point rating scale. Survey questions were developed to address each learning outcome. The highest-rated outcomes involved those aspects of the first-year advising program that occurred primarily within an individual advising session with the student (such as goal setting and educational planning). The lowest-rated outcomes involved those aspects of the program that were presented primarily within an advisor-led group presentation and involved a rather passive approach to learning (understanding college policies and procedures, awareness of services and resources).

Overall, the results of the assessment project indicate that participation in the first-year advising program contributes to aspects of student learning that are necessary for development of self-directed learners. Clearly, students are not expected to become self-directed learners in the course of one initial advising session. However, the results can be used to identify those areas in which students will need additional and continuous reinforcement in order to develop the learning outcomes that characterize self-directed learners.

As a result of the assessment results, several specific actions were identified to improve the advising process:

- Enhance the career development component of the first-year advising program. An interactive module allowing students to engage in an online career assessment has been developed and will be added to the program in 2007.
- Increase emphasis on instructing students how to select general education courses.

NEW DIRECTIONS FOR STUDENT SERVICES • DOI: 10.1002/ss

Figure 3.1. Counseling and Advising Outcomes Assessment Template

AREA: Student Development/Counseling and Advising

GOAL/OBJECTIVE: Students will become self-directed learners

EXPECTED OUTCOMES

1.1 Students will demonstrate knowledge of academic requirements (e.g., curriculum requirements for their intended program, general education, etc.)

1.2 Students will articulate an educational and career goal

1.3 Students will develop an educational plan outlining steps necessary to reach their educational goals

1.4 Students will demonstrate awareness of how to access college resources and services

1.5 Students will demonstrate knowledge of educational policies and procedures

MEASUREMENT	BENCHMARK	ASSESSMENT TOOL
1.1–1.5 Student rating of effectiveness of first-year advising session in developing skills necessary for becoming self-directed learners	3.7 mean score for each survey item addressing each outcome	Survey to be administered to all first-year advising session participants

STRATEGIES	ASSIGNED TO
1.1–1.5 Continue use of ICAP forms (Individual College Academic Plans), which focus on development of self-directed learner skills	All advisors in Student Development Target date: ongoing
1.1–1.5 Reformat new student advising information to continue focus on development of self-directed learner skills, and highlight topics such as general education courses, use of Degree Progress Report, transfer planning, and online student account access	Director of counseling and advising and Student Development Target date: begin reformatted process in May 2007
1.4 Offer sessions in conjunction with the WRC to teach students how to use online account access for self-registration, academic planning, etc.	Counseling and advising staff and WRC staff Target date: spring 2007

STATUS/FEEDBACK LOOP (How have data been used to enhance learning, services, processes?)

1. First-year advising session to be reformatted to enhance career development component

2. Increase opportunities to instruct students how to select general education courses in Advising Guide, semester schedule

3. Implement registration module in first-year advising session to instruct students in course registration policies and procedures

NEW DIRECTIONS FOR STUDENT SERVICES • DOI: 10.1002/ss

- Increase emphasis in the first-year advising program on review of college policies and procedures related to the registration process.

Tips for Implementing the Process

Implementing a comprehensive assessment process for any organization is challenging. From Frederick Community College's experience, we offer these tips, which may be helpful in guiding implementation of an assessment process:

- Provide professional development on assessment of student learning for staff. Early on at FCC, we realized that staff understanding of the assessment process ranged from little to fairly sophisticated knowledge of assessing learning. Closing the knowledge gap was essential to move the process forward.
- Involve staff at the beginning to facilitate buy-in to the assessment process.
- Furnishing the "template" really helped staff understand the differences among goal, objective, outcome, measurement or benchmark, and strategy.
- Encourage staff to read the literature on assessment of student learning.
- Make available time to do the work.
- Keep the process as streamlined and simple as possible.

Overcoming Barriers to Assessing Student Learning and Development

Significant resources are required to sustain a comprehensive assessment of student learning program. Commitment of staff time and investment in professional development to ensure adequate skills in assessment techniques and data analysis is necessary and accounts for a significant amount of program time. To leverage resources, Learning Support uses sources of data from other offices on campus, particularly the Institutional Research Office, to evaluate established student learning outcomes. By inventorying the full range of evaluations and assessments conducted throughout the campus, Learning Support programs were able to identify those assessments relevant to the learning outcomes being examined in their area.

Also, Learning Support programs have been able to add locally developed survey items to standardized assessment instruments administered by the college. For example, when administering the Community College Survey of Student Engagement, the Institutional Research Office incorporated several questions developed to assess learning outcomes–related academic advising, thus allowing the Advising Office to evaluate student achievement of learning outcomes with resources leveraged through an existing survey.

Assessment efforts at FCC continue to develop and mature. Future plans include additional staff development bringing in an outside consultant to assist staff in expanding use of learning-based outcomes and linking Learning Support's assessment outcomes to the college's general education program outcomes.

References

American College Personnel Association. *The Student Learning Imperative: Implications for Student Affairs*. Washington, D.C.: American College Personnel Association, 1996. Retrieved Jan. 30, 2007, from http://www.acpa.nche.edu/sli/sli.htm.

American College Personnel Association, and National Association of Student Personnel Administrators. *Principles of Good Practice for Student Affairs*. Washington, D.C.: ACPA, NASPA, 1997.

American College Personnel Association, and National Association of Student Personnel Administrators. *Learning Reconsidered: A Campus-wide Focus on the Student Experience*. Washington, D.C.: ACPA, NASPA, 2004.

Bresciani, M. J. "Outcomes Assessment in Student Affairs: Moving Beyond Satisfaction to Student Learning and Development." *National Association for Student Personnel Administrators Net RESULTS E-Zine*, 2002. Retrieved Feb. 15, 2007, from http://www.naspa.org.

O'Banion, T. *A Learning College for the 21st Century*. American Council on Education/ Oryx Press Series on Higher Education. Phoenix, Ariz.: Oryx Press, 1997.

L. RICHARD HANEY serves as the vice president for learning support and interim executive director of institutional advancement at Frederick Community College.

DEBRALEE MCCLELLAN is the associate vice president for student development at Frederick Community College.

NEW DIRECTIONS FOR STUDENT SERVICES • DOI: 10.1002/ss

4

This chapter provides a glimpse of student affairs assessment at Isothermal Community College including a specific example of assessment, tips to implementing assessment at your institution, and barriers encountered when implementing the process at Isothermal Community College.

Isothermal Community College

Karen Kitchens Jones

Overview of Institutional Culture

Isothermal Community College (ICC) is located in Spindale, North Carolina. The college serves approximately two thousand curriculum students every fall and spring semester and about one thousand curriculum students in summer semesters. Students come from all walks of life, with goals that range from high school or GED completion to college transfer as a stepping stone to a bachelor's degree and beyond. ICC's curriculum program is organized into four academic areas: arts and sciences (including nursing), business sciences, applied sciences and technology, and developmental education.

Beginning in the mid-1990s and continuing to date, the college reexamined its mission and philosophy and continues a transformation in culture from the teaching paradigm to the learning paradigm. The vision is to transform the college into a preeminent center recognized nationally for excellence in learning and services. A significant vehicle for progress in this area has been formation of the Team for the Advancement of the Learning College (TALC), which functions as an umbrella organization furnishing resources and guidance for a variety of taskforces seeking to promote a focus on learning at ICC. These work teams consist of volunteers from throughout the campus and cover the areas of professional development, learning strategies, enhancing systems and processes, campus life, institutional effectiveness, business and industry training, academic advising, and assessment.

NEW DIRECTIONS FOR STUDENT SERVICES, no. 127, Fall 2009 © Wiley Periodicals, Inc.
Published online in Wiley InterScience (www.interscience.wiley.com) • DOI: 10.1002/ss.325

Overview of Division of Student Affairs/Services

The Student Affairs department at ICC is divided into ten functional areas. Over the last several years, student affairs staff thought carefully about how their areas support learning, and each area articulated student learning outcomes. Learning outcomes provide the guidance needed for staff to address what their areas are seeking to accomplish, why these accomplishments are important, and whether or not their efforts are working. Satisfaction outcomes continue to be important to student affairs staff, and satisfaction outcome statements are articulated.

The functional areas employ a variety of techniques to assess learning and satisfaction outcome achievement. Every year, staff set aside time to reflect on what has been learned through assessment, compile related documents into a portfolio, and summarize major areas of learning into what we refer to as "reflective narratives." The process is systematic and ongoing, with portfolios and narratives submitted for review by various administrators in June of that year.

Overview of the Assessment Process

An important beginning step for any assessment plan is consideration of the college and departmental mission. Thus, when a more comprehensive assessment process was proposed for the Student Affairs department in March 2003, we agreed that a departmental mission was needed to support and encourage the larger mission of improving life through learning. Consequently, the departmental mission statement was brainstormed in staff meetings, and this mission was adopted by the group: "The mission of the Student Affairs department is to support the learning college environment through the provision of services and programs that are inviting, user-friendly, accessible, and designed to facilitate student development and learning."

Assessment: Past and Present. We have a long history of active engagement in assessment activities. These efforts yielded a wealth of information to guide decision making within the department and throughout the college. Assessment documents in Student Affairs date back to the late 1980s, when preparations were taking place for the 1993 program review. During this time, most assessment feedback was garnered through surveys of students.

It is also important to note that Student Affairs staff engaged in a number of other meaningful activities related to assessment during the same time frame. For example, we contributed to two accreditation miniaudits, several learning college retreats devoted to brainstorming and problem solving, and development of rubrics to evaluate learning in the instructional domain. Student Affairs staff also benefited from information gleaned from

NEW DIRECTIONS FOR STUDENT SERVICES • DOI: 10.1002/ss

the Faces of the Future and Community College Survey of Student Engagement (CCSSE) surveys, which revealed important shifts in the profile of ICC's student population as well as important information related to student engagement.

Also, we identified staff needs and comfort level with tasks related to assessment as result of a needs analysis and a pre- and postsurvey of assessment learning conducted by the graduate researcher. The needs analysis revealed an overall positive desire on the part of Student Affairs staff to learn more about assessment. It also reinforced what we already knew regarding staff concerns about heavy workloads. At the same time, a comparison of staff's pre- and postscores showed positive increases in these categories: (1) comfort level with assessment, (2) knowledge of assessment, (3) skill in executing assessment, and (4) progress in assessment efforts. Overall, the most significant contribution of the graduate researcher is development of some concrete steps to aid in assessment efforts. The department has learned that assessment involves processes that are fluid, abstract, and dynamic, which makes it inherently difficult to understand.

Here is a partial summary of activities that we have undertaken since 2003 in developing an assessment plan for Student Affairs:

1. Establish departmental and functional area mission statements.
2. Review survey results and student feedback continuously, along with other sources of information (e.g., focus group results, benchmarking, peer review).
3. Consider summative departmental reports (e.g., numbers that reveal trends, provide insight).
4. Explore objectives (main purposes) that are consistent with the mission.
5. Develop expected outcomes that are measurable or identifiable in terms of numbers (e.g., use of services), satisfaction outcomes, and learning outcomes.
6. Consider how evaluation methods could be more closely tied to outcomes in developing specific plans.
7. Collect and review data on an ongoing basis.
8. Close the loop by documenting improvements through one-step or multistep methods and providing interpretation of the data (e.g., reflective narrative).
9. Repeat process.
10. Seek help and further training in support of assessment!

Portfolios in Student Affairs. As these efforts were cultivated across the Student Affairs area, it has become necessary to develop systems for managing assessment information. Consequently, staff members are compiling assessment information into functional area portfolios, which are submitted for review annually in June. The information in these portfolios seeks to answer seven questions for each functional area:

1. What are the essential services provided by the functional area?
2. How does the functional area support the college and departmental mission?
3. What data are available regarding use of functional area services?
4. What data are available that indicate whether or not students and others are satisfied with this area of service?
5. What data are available that demonstrate whether or not this service area supports learning?
6. How does available assessment information influence important decisions, improvements, and changes in this service area?
7. What developments are on the horizon for this service area?

All functional areas are engaged in data collection and interpretation related to numbers (for example, use of services), satisfaction (on the part of students and faculty), and learning. Staff in each functional area manage assessment portfolios, which have five sections:

1. A statement of mission for the functional area, along with outcome statements for numbers, satisfaction, and learning
2. A description of essential categories and main purposes for the functional area
3. Assessment plans
4. Quality improvement documentation
5. Reflective narratives

The most compelling dimension of the portfolio is the reflective narrative, which describes what has been learned in the previous year as a result of assessment results. The aim of the reflective narrative is to describe learning related to assessment and address the seven questions indicated in the earlier list.

Functional area portfolios are maintained at the functional area level and are backed up electronically on the Student Affairs server. This information is compiled annually into a larger document that is housed in the office of the Dean of Student Affairs and shared with the Office of Assessment, Research, and Planning, the college administration, and others expressing interest.

It is also important to note here that this process has resulted in development of many additional assessment strategies. These strategies as well as others are detailed in functional area assessment plans and are certain to expand in the future as we assume meaningful roles in the collegewide assessment taskforce, which is seeking to better integrate academic and ser-

NEW DIRECTIONS FOR STUDENT SERVICES • DOI: 10.1002/ss

vice area assessment as well as consider how students may be more involved in the assessment process.

Example of Assessment and How Results Are Used

The financial aid office furnished an example of assessment. Learning outcomes for the office are that:

- ICC students will demonstrate an awareness of financial aid services.
- ICC students will gain an understanding of the financial aid processes that they must navigate in order for them to receive financial aid.
- Financial aid staff will understand financial aid issues, procedures, and regulations.

A student satisfaction outcome related to financial aid: Financial aid students will report that financial aid services are inviting, people-centered, accessible, and designed to facilitate student development and learning.

We believe that financial aid is vitally important in making higher education accessible within our service region. A first step is facilitating awareness about financial aid opportunities. Awareness is important, because many of our students are first-generation college students who may not be aware of available financial aid. Our objective is to facilitate learning on their part about financial assistance that may be available to them.

A next step is to facilitate learning about financial aid processes so that an increasing number of students can navigate the process and receive the aid they need to attend college. We think that financial aid can be overwhelming and complicated. This may be especially true for first-generation college students. Of course, at the same time we also hope that our financial aid staff will prove themselves to be well trained and that students will be pleased with the services they receive.

There are many methods for assessing learning and student satisfaction outcomes statements related to financial aid. They include survey and focus group feedback and the percentage of the ICC student body receiving financial aid. Benchmarking data are also considered: Pell disbursement compared to institutions of similar size in North Carolina, national trends related to the average amount of financial aid disbursed in public two-year colleges, and so on.

Financial aid can play a key role in helping students overcome access barriers associated with financial need. In this regard, many decisions have been made at ICC to contribute toward the achievement of student learning about financial aid and related processes. Staffing has been enhanced, the travel budget has increased significantly, and many processes related to how the office facilitates student learning about financial aid have been completely revamped.

Tips for Implementing the Process

It is important to remember that development of a meaningful assessment plan takes time, training, and collaboration. The first priority in engaging staff in assessment efforts is setting aside time for assessment. At ICC this would not be possible without the support of the administration, which allots ongoing resources to support part-time staff persons in covering the office. Having staff in place to cover offices has enabled the entire full-time staff to meet regularly to engage in assessment tasks, training, and the like. We believe that this broad-based participation among all staff is essential in making assessment part of the fabric of departmental life and cultivating buy-in for assessment in student services. Also, we acknowledge that support for conference attendance, outside consulting, and guidance from our own assessment office have proven instrumental in moving our department forward.

We have also learned how to better manage the information gleaned from assessment. It is important to resist the temptation to react every time negative information is received. We like to think of this better approach as looking for the "crowd," as opposed to the "critic." The crowd represents the feedback we receive over and over that highlights the need to adapt services and programs to better achieve student learning. As we become better able to interpret what we learn from assessment, the trends and patterns are more apparent. At the same time, the need to overreact to the occasional, isolated critic is much less tempting.

Our most practical lessons, however, pertain to the nuts-and-bolts approach to assessment. This is the easy stuff that we most often overlook. In order to promote creativity on the part of all functional areas, we neglected some important steps until rather late in the process:

1. We created definitions for terms related to assessment and agreed to refer to these terms consistently.
2. We developed a uniform approach to organizing assessment portfolios.
3. We identified a central location to store electronic documents related to assessment.
4. We agreed on a specific time frame for assessment due dates every year.
5. We identified titles for all surveys and agreed to refer to this survey feedback uniformly.

Yet another practical and notable lesson was determining that it is not possible to assess everything simultaneously. Last but not least, we need to make sure that assessment plans are read! Reflective narratives from each functional area are compiled annually into one document for routing to the president, vice presidents, assessment director, and others as deemed appropriate. Specific feedback from these parties demonstrates to staff that their work is reviewed. When assessment information is used in decision making or for resource allocation, it is important that staff know what is happening. Also, we recognize that assessment creates opportunities for "internal and external outreach." Accordingly, student affairs staff seize opportunities to present information related to assessment activities at collegewide assessment meetings, area conferences, and workshops.

Overcoming Barriers to Assessing Student Learning and Development

A focus on learning requires a paradigm shift for those accustomed to operating in a "doing" mode versus a "reflecting" mode. This shift reflects a change from assessing the number of students served to what students are learning as a result of services. Student affairs staff persons have long been accustomed to being busy every minute of the day and working hard to meet student needs. However, student affairs staff at ICC have not previously been asked to evaluate how their efforts have an impact on learning. Evaluation of learning requires forethought in establishing learning outcomes, assessing learning outcomes, reflecting on learning outcome achievement on the part of students served, and carefully planning improvements based on outcome achievement. Accordingly, time spent in thoughtful planning and reflection is vitally important in the student affairs assessment process. This is a big adjustment for staff who may have viewed time spent thinking and planning as time wasted "sitting around" when there were students to see and phones to answer. Thanks to training, administrators who lead by example, and much encouragement, staff are gradually becoming more accustomed to the reflection that is inseparable from the assessment process. Anecdotal reports from staff indicate that the rewards are a more proactive approach to their work, a fuller understanding of their role in the college, and a more nuanced understanding of how they can help students succeed.

Another developmental area in the ICC student affairs assessment journey has been learning to manage negative feedback. It seems that staff struggle with bad news. Although this subject has not been studied from a scientific standpoint, it appears that student services personnel often have a "heart and soul" approach to their work and operate with the best intentions in serving students. It just plain hurts when assessment yields bad news. To combat this difficulty, we are working to make it "safe" to reveal weaknesses in programs and services. In order to convince staff of this, we are attempting to view problems as opportunities for learning and seeking to provide the support necessary to address challenges in a manner that is positive, constructive, and supportive of student learning.

Overall, the most formidable assessment challenge encountered by Student Affairs would have to be staff turnover. Since a more comprehensive assessment process was implemented, several staff moved into other jobs. In some cases, staff expansion has resulted in shifting assessment responsibilities within the department. These changes allow the department to continue to benefit from staff knowledge of and experience with assessment. Unfortunately, however, in several instances the department lost valuable expertise (including two enrollment management directors and two testing coordinators) to neighboring community colleges. Each new hire requires orientation to the assessment process and much training. These transitions do not always correspond conveniently to training opportunities, which often mean that training must be conducted one-on-one.

There is no doubt that cultivating a plan for assessment of learning is an ongoing, time-consuming, and often daunting task. Assessment of student learning is a task with no specific start or end date. Rather, it involves circular processes with loops opening and closing all the time. It will always be necessary to acquaint new people with assessment procedures, but it is an invigorating journey that yields meaningful information regarding how student services efforts contribute to the learning college setting. As the learning college movement evolves, it will become increasingly important that student services staff find and articulate their place in the learning college.

KAREN KITCHENS JONES is dean of student affairs at Isothermal Community College (ICC).

NEW DIRECTIONS FOR STUDENT SERVICES • DOI: 10.1002/ss

5

This chapter provides a glimpse of student affairs assessment at John Carroll University including a specific example of assessment, tips to implementing assessment at your institution, and barriers encountered when implementing the process at John Carroll University.

John Carroll University

Kathleen Lis Dean, Patrick Rombalski, Kyle O'Dell

Overview of Institutional Culture

John Carroll University is a Jesuit Catholic institution located in University Heights, approximately ten miles east of Cleveland, Ohio. Founded in 1888, the university has a population of thirty-four hundred undergraduates and eight hundred graduate students. The undergraduate enrollment is overwhelmingly made up of traditional-age students between eighteen and twenty-two years old. Fifty-four percent of the student body comes from Northeastern Ohio, 72 percent of the students are Catholic, and 9 percent of the undergraduate students are minority. The university has an 85 percent retention rate and a 76 percent five-year graduation rate.

The Jesuit ideal of *magis*, or seeking of the "more," guides our assessment efforts as we strive to understand and educate our students. This means we seek excellence in all that we do by setting high standards for our students and ourselves. Assessment allows us to reflect on the extent to which we are meeting these standards as we consider the effectiveness of our programs and services and understand how we can improve. By incorporating assessment into our ongoing work and our strategic planning process, we monitor progress toward our goals. We are committed to integrating assessment into our work as a means to guide decision making, communicate progress, and understand the impact of our work in service of the mission.

NEW DIRECTIONS FOR STUDENT SERVICES, no. 127, Fall 2009 © Wiley Periodicals, Inc.
Published online in Wiley InterScience (www.interscience.wiley.com) • DOI: 10.1002/ss.326

Overview of Division of Student Affairs

The Division of Student Affairs comprises eleven units. The mission of the division is the same as that of the university: to develop women and men who have the knowledge and character to lead and to serve. Members of the John Carroll campus community have varying expectations of Student Affairs. At one end of the continuum, many faculty members are "educationally conservative," believing that the rest of the university exists solely to support the academic mission. These individuals view the division purely as a "student life" function and understand us as an auxiliary service that focuses on coordinating social activities and delivering services.

At the other end of the spectrum, there are some faculty members and academic administrators at John Carroll who do acknowledge the need to create a seamless learning environment in collaboration with Student Affairs. These individuals see an opportunity for student learning to occur both inside and outside the classroom, believing that learning is an institutional responsibility and that all members of the campus community should work together to accomplish this goal. This group characterizes their expectations for the division as ensuring that students have access to "channels of engagement." This means our expected role is to create an environment in which classroom learning is extended into other aspects of students' lives and enables students to become connected, involved, and engaged in ways that lead toward the ultimate goal of student success.

Overview of the Assessment Process

Assessment in the division takes place within and across departments. The assistant vice president directs the overall assessment process for assessment and planning in Student Affairs. Although the division has primarily relied on several national surveys to date (CIRP, CSS, NSSE, SSI, Core, NCHA), we also develop and implement more local approaches to assessment, including departmentally developed surveys, rubrics, and focus groups.

Data from these surveys are shared both within the division and across the campus through several outlets. Raw data, primarily in the form of frequencies, and executive summaries of surveys are stored on an intranet site accessible to all departments within the division. The assessment website also holds reference to many aspects of our developing program, including information about surveys in which we participate, updates on current projects, interesting data points, divisional learning outcomes, and links to other useful student affairs websites.

The divisional efforts also include an assessment team with a representative from each department, a graduate student, and an undergraduate student. The mission of the assessment team is to furnish education, guidance, and resources for assessment by assisting with the assessment process, creating and implementing an assessment timeline, assisting with creation of departmental assessment plans, promoting active engagement of all members of the division in assessing student learning, maintaining ongoing conversations about student learning outcomes and the merit of assessment within Student Affairs, and encouraging understanding of assessment throughout the division. The division is also engaged in assessment processes at the university level through membership on the university assessment committee.

A majority of the departments submit assessment plans. Assessment plans give staff the opportunity to reflect on their purpose and goals, and to convey a hierarchy of ideas as they relate to intended outcomes. Starting this past year, rather than reporting assessment results as a stand-alone document, departments were asked to integrate this information into a year-end report that included basic information about their department, best practices, new initiatives, and challenges. This report was intended to be a helpful and necessary opportunity to reflect on departmental work over the past year. Using a rubric, members of the Student Affairs Assessment Team annually review assessment plans and reports.

During the last year, the division intentionally wrote outcome statements into its strategic plan. This will connect information to the particular issues and goals we are trying to address and achieve. By incorporating ongoing assessment into implementation of the strategic plan, we can monitor progress toward our goals and continuously refine our programs and policies. With a mix of departmental and divisional projects, assessment plays an ongoing role in the strategic planning process by measuring our success and answering the question, "How will we know?" Assessment is not the end but rather the means to understand and accomplish our goals. In other words, assessment is in service of the mission.

The model in Figure 5.1 shows how we view integration of the strategic plan and the assessment process. The process started with the JCU and

Figure 5.1. The Role of Assessment in Strategic Planning

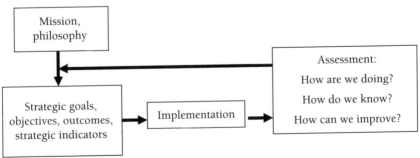

Source: Model adapted from Freeman, Bresciani, and Bresciani (2004) and St. Onge and Wells (2004).

divisional mission and how we approach our work from a philosophical perspective. These ideas serve as a foundation for the work of our division and help to determine appropriate strategic goals. Statements of both our objectives as student affairs professionals and our expectations for student outcomes have emerged from goal statements.

The division's five-year strategic plan outlines three primary goals, each highlighting Student Affairs' role in student learning:

1. Cultivation of the student experience
2. Development of our students' character
3. Their engagement in the civic life of their communities

Each goal contains specific objectives and measurable outcomes to help us determine our progress.

Example of Assessment and How Results Are Used

The Office of Residence Life recently conducted an assessment project in response to an increased level of negative behavior in the residence halls, including vandalism and disrespectful behavior. This project was an ideal opportunity to understand how we could address social issues in our residential learning environment. National calls for character education were also influential in the decision to address this issue. This project was designed to address the effectiveness of a character education initiative (CEI) in the residence halls.

A brief survey was distributed to all residential students who attended their floor meetings during the month of April. Students were asked to indicate which passive character education efforts they had noticed and then indicate to what degree the materials had changed their beliefs and behaviors. The goal of this assessment project was to answer a group of questions related to character education:

1. Are resident students reading the posted character education materials?
2. Do students feel their personal beliefs and behaviors have changed as a result of the character education materials?
3. Do students perceive that the behavior of other resident students has changed as a result of the character education materials?
4. Is there a relationship among gender, year in school, and hall of residence in CEI-related behavior and the perceived behaviors of others on campus?

These data resulted in several findings. First, the data suggested that there were both gender differences and class-year differences in responses. For example, female residents were more likely to report having read the materials referenced. The survey results also indicated that first-year students were the most likely to report having read them, while junior students were least likely to have done so.

This assessment project afforded insight regarding how students receive information as well as how passive initiatives might affect perceived behaviors and beliefs. From these findings, different approaches will be used for first-year residence halls and those that house sophomore, junior, and senior students. These assessment results helped to inform the residence life staff about how to best communicate with students, identified a need to do things differently with first-year students and continuing students, identified what information works passively rather than actively, and lent evidence that students can be influenced by such materials.

This assessment project resulted in several programmatic and policy changes. First, it helped to inform an overall change in the residence life curriculum model. The new model intentionally treats programming for upper-class students differently from that for first-year students, rather than viewing the educational needs of all residents as the same. Second, the content of the residence life newsletter, *HallBeat*, was also modified to include more intentional information on educational topics. Finally, these results also changed the programming expectations for resident assistants (RAs). The previous model allowed residence hall staff to implement whatever programming they wanted, so long as they accumulated a certain number of points each semester. The new model has specific goals and guidelines to be followed regarding populations and topic and conveys the importance of addressing aspects of character education differently according to type of student. For example, the issue of alcohol use should be treated differently for first-year students (for example, information about policies and risks) than for older students of legal drinking age (a "mocktail" program). Master's-level area coordinators drive programming in the new curricular model, reflecting their higher level of student development knowledge.

Tips for Implementing the Process

Although we are still in the very early stages of our strategic plan, there are some lessons to pass along. Perhaps most important, we incorporated a role for assessment into the strategic plan through use of goals, objectives, and student outcomes. We are still learning, but we encourage other student affairs divisions to duplicate this effort; it has established a solid basis for understanding and communicating what is important to our division and will serve us as a roadmap for measuring our progress.

As we approach the end of the second year, divisional data and results from department assessment projects are being reviewed and synthesized to produce a developing picture of where we are and where we need to go. In addition, we are beginning a program audit project (Taylor and Matney, 2007) that will review all of the division's programs and services to understand how they fit into the strategic plan. Departments will be asked to identify who their programs serve, when, and in collaboration with whom, as well as which outcomes they are intentionally designed to address. The goal of this project is to understand what the division is already doing and how we might more intentionally connect programs and services. We would highly recommend other divisions undertake this type of project earlier in a strategic planning cycle in order to inform decision making.

Furthermore, development of the strategic goals was an iterative and inclusive process taking place over several months with the participation of multiple representatives from all departments and from different levels of responsibility. By involving so many people from a variety of areas, they are able to understand the foundational role of assessment in the strategic plan and, more important, align their departmental initiatives and assessment projects with the divisional goals.

A final piece of advice for managing the process is to focus preliminary assessment efforts on departments that are better equipped and more capable from a resource and expertise perspective. So much of incorporating assessment into the life of an organization is generating buy-in. By working closely with those who are likely to be ambassadors and role models, those who are resistant or less capable will have more reason to follow.

Overcoming Barriers to Assessing Student Learning and Development

Our division struggles with three clear barriers: location of several "nontraditional" departments within our division, knowledge of assessment that is still in its infancy for most professionals in the division, and limited staff. The challenge lies in that the staff members in these areas are not trained in student affairs or higher education, so the language of assessment and student development is less accessible. Furthermore, we are one of only a very few Jesuit institutions with a dedicated assessment person within the Division of Student Affairs, so there are few or no colleagues who face similar situations. However, we are beginning to overcome this in two ways. One approach we have used is to fully include staff members in the assessment process and in efforts to educate all staff about the benefits of assessment. Second, we have been able to acknowledge how these departments contribute to student learning, as well as to other factors such as engagement and retention, particularly through the lens of our strategic plan. We hope to share our experience with similar institutions and begin conversation around our common missions and the role of assessment.

A second challenge is the still-developing knowledge of assessment within the division. In particular, staff members are not yet comfortable with the focus on learning outcomes and are often at a loss about how to use data once they collect them. Although the focus is growing, it still exists in pockets primarily, in areas with larger numbers of staff with degrees in student affairs. As stated previously, one strategy has been to rely on these offices from a low-hanging-fruit approach. In other words, we have identified potential champions among those staff members and offices already engaged in some level of assessment or who have expressed interest in assessment. However, there are several other strategies we are using to work with the knowledge barrier. First, incorporation of outcomes into the strategic plan has helped to bring the concept of assessment to the forefront of departmental attention. Learning outcomes in particular have been emphasized throughout and are quickly becoming the coin of the realm. As we move further along with the strategic plan, reports of our progress in these areas will become increasingly highlighted. Integrating assessment reports into the end-of-the-year reports will further serve to highlight the importance of assessment and help staff realize how this information is integrated into the life of their offices.

A second strategy related to the knowledge barrier was to invite a representative from every office engaged in assessment to join the Student Affairs Assessment Team, rather than only those who previously showed interest. Finally, as with many campuses, we have limited staff to manage the assessment process. Many of the strategies listed here begin to address this issue by moving responsibility for assessment down the hierarchy, but the role of assessment education is still prominent. Sharing data and resources via the website, incorporating assessment into existing processes, and using the potential power of the assessment team does begin to address this issue. Continuing to educate and offer support will help to diminish the significance of this barrier, as will the growing number of professionals who graduate with some knowledge of assessment in student affairs.

References

Freeman, J. P., Bresciani, M. J., and Bresciani, D. "Integrated Strategic Planning: Bringing Planning and Assessment Together." *National Association for Student Personnel Administrators Net RESULTS E-Zine*, 2004. Retrieved Sept. 25, 2006, from http://www.naspa.org/membership/mem/nr/article.cfm?id=1327.

St. Onge, S., and Wells, B. L. "Assessment Strategic Planning: Getting the Most out of Your Assessment Plan." *National Association for Student Personnel Administrators Net RESULTS E-Zine*, 2004. Retrieved Sept. 25, 2006, from http://www.naspa.org/membership/mem/nr/article.cfm?id=1302.

Taylor, S. H., and Matney, M. M. "Transforming Student Affairs Strategic Planning into Tangible Results." *NASPA Journal*, 2007, 44(1).

KATHLEEN LIS DEAN *is the assistant vice president for assessment and planning in student affairs at John Carroll University (JCU).*

PATRICK ROMBALSKI *is the vice president for student affairs at Boston College and former VPSA at JCU.*

KYLE O'DELL *is the coordinator for orientation at John Carroll University.*

6

*This chapter provides a glimpse of student affairs assess-
ment at Northern Arizona University including a specific
example of assessment, tips to implementing assessment
at your institution, and barriers encountered when implementing the process at Northern Arizona University.*

Northern Arizona University

*Michael F. Butcher, Margot Saltonstall, Sarah Bickel,
Rick Brandel*

Overview of Institutional Culture

NAU is a public university nestled below the San Francisco Peaks in
Flagstaff, Arizona. It enrolls more than twenty-one thousand undergraduate and graduate students at its main campus in Flagstaff, through its thirty-
five statewide sites, and via online program offerings. This university offers
ninety-five undergraduate degrees, forty-seven master's degrees, and eight
doctoral degrees. NAU pursues a delicate balance among teaching, scholarship, and service with faculty and staff dedicated to each student's success.
The university is classified by the Carnegie Foundation as a large, comprehensive, doctoral, high undergraduate, primarily residential university with
a high level of research activity. With its main campus in Flagstaff, NAU is
the only public university located in northern Arizona's rural region ("Self-
Study Draft," 2007).

Overview of Division of Student Affairs/Services

Within the university organizational system, Student Affairs has a prominent position. Recently, Enrollment Management and Student Affairs
(EMSA) departments combined to create one division. The vice president
for enrollment management and student affairs reports directly to the president of Northern Arizona University. The vice president for enrollment

management and student affairs directly supervises two associate vice presidents for enrollment management and student affairs, the associate vice president for student affairs, the associate vice president of enrollment services, and the director of residence life.

The division has the role of serving the diverse students of the university. Located in the Southwest, Northern Arizona University attracts a unique population of Native American and Hispanic students. Northern Arizona University ranks fifth in the nation for graduating Native Americans with bachelor's degrees, according to the 2006 ranking in *Diverse Issues in Higher Education* magazine ("Top 100," 2006). Within EMSA, Native American Student Services (NASS) is committed to providing culturally sensitive support services to NAU's Native American and Alaskan Native students as part of the university's mission. The emphasis is on serving first-year freshmen and transfer students and offering assistance with the transition from home to the university community. The students represent or have represented more than fifty tribes throughout the United States.

Overview of the Assessment Process

The mission of Student Affairs is to promote academic and personal success. Within the university and the communities it serves, Student Affairs partners to offer student-centered programs and services, valuing student learning, diversity, and responsible citizenship. Beginning in orientation, students are encouraged to take advantage of the many programs and services made available on campus. Involvement in student organizations, internships and practicums, and student employment create opportunities for student learning to occur outside of the classroom. Additionally, examples of contexts within which student learning occurs include the Learning Assistance Centers, residence halls and Residence Life programs, and clubs and organizations. The Learning Assistance Centers offer free tutoring and focus on helping students become independent learners. The residential Learning Communities within Residence Life give students the opportunity to connect with others on the basis of common interests or career goals. Participation in student organizations and clubs gives students the ability to work with others to build teams and develop their own leadership potential. Essentially, these programs and services help to build the importance of creating connections on campus.

Student Affairs staff understand the need to build strong faculty connections. Faculty participation is critical to the operation of the University Hearing Board, the Residence Life Learning Communities, and on advisory boards for many Student Affairs departments. In addition, several faculty members were recently consulted on development of an ethnic-minority survey, which aimed to collect information that would be used to better some students inside and outside the classroom. Faculty are more invested when they are involved in assessment from the beginning. One area in which faculty involvement in Student Affairs at NAU is growing is in assessment.

Developing an Assessment Program. Planning for a comprehensive Student Affairs assessment program began in the spring of 1996. The new leadership within Student Affairs was seeking to articulate program effectiveness and determine appropriate resource allocation. At that time, there was a strong sense among Student Affairs staff that their programs were effective; yet they had little evidence to support their beliefs. This was the impetus for assessment planning efforts.

The assessment model as initially implemented was based on the research of M. Lee Upcraft and John H. Schuh. In their pivotal book *Assessment in Student Affairs: A Guide for Practitioners* (1996), Upcraft and Schuh present a guide to development of a comprehensive assessment program. The Student Affairs leadership at NAU drew from many of Upcraft and Schuh's ideas in creating the foundations of the assessment program.

In these early years, Student Affairs leadership understood that they were setting the initial tone for assessment, which would eventually communicate the purpose of assessment for all of Student Affairs (Erwin, 1991). Therefore, developing a core understanding of assessment that could be adapted to the various departments was imperative to the success of assessment in Student Affairs. Embracing and emphasizing the importance of developing a comprehensive assessment program contributed to the success of the assessment program that continues today. It was essential to include stakeholders to support and participate in assessment. In addition, assessment questions cannot be fully addressed without participation by students, student affairs leadership, and others in the educational community. The early conversations about assessment were collaborative discussions among Student Affairs leaders, which yielded the assessment coordinator position, enabling a full-time staff member to devote all of her or his time to assessment activities. Collaboration has been one of the cornerstones that continue to contribute to its success. The assessment coordinator now leads that collaborative effort.

Current Assessment Structure and Processes. Currently, a full-time enrollment management and student affairs assessment coordinator, two graduate assistants, and a team of departmental representatives lead assessment efforts. The coordinator takes a lead role in communicating why assessment is carried out and thereby translates internal and external pressures to conduct assessment, into meaningful incentives (Saltonstall, 2006). Additionally, the coordinator facilitates an assessment team. This Assessment Resource Team is composed of at least one representative from all the departments within the division. The team meets regularly to discuss departmental and divisional assessment projects.

In addition to the Assessment Resource Team, Student Affairs departments participate on the Divisional Strategic Planning Committee. These groups work together to create departmental strategic plans that identify priorities and include assessment components. To walk through the process of identifying departmental priorities, departmental representatives complete a form called Plans for Departmental Priorities and Their Assessment, which requires them to describe accompanying assessment measure(s).

Evaluating the departmental priorities plan is an instrumental step in the assessment process for EMSA departments. The priorities plan is evaluated to determine if the activities, objectives, and assessments are appropriate. A rubric is used to examine each departmental priority. The criteria contained in the rubric used to evaluate priorities are that:

- The objective clearly articulates with named EMSA goal(s).
- The activity is programmatic.
- The activity is well defined, including who will be served or targeted.
- Outcomes stated are appropriate measure(s) of activity.
- Assessment is manageable.

All of these criterion points are measured on a scale of "not at all," "develop further," and "no changes needed." There is also a section for comments. Once all of the departmental priorities are evaluated, the reviewers consider the overall plan of priorities submitted. Using a yes-or-no scale, the criteria that the reviewers use to evaluate the overall plan are:

- Overall, the plan seems manageable for the department.
- Assessment includes a combination of participation and use, satisfaction, and learning outcomes data.
- The key players include an appropriate mix of staff, faculty, and students.

Finally, the reviewers note the overall strengths of the plan along with key areas to improve. Each departmental representative receives a copy of the completed evaluation rubric for her or his plan in order to make any needed changes, as well as to reflect on strengths and other comments noted. This process functions to increase the Strategic Planning Committee members' awareness of others' priorities and concomitant assessment measures, which in turn increases the knowledge within the division in terms of common objectives, unique contribution to EMSA goals, and assessment strategies and methods. It also allows each individual unit to get feedback from peers.

The EMSA leadership is flexible in creating and supporting employee developed assessment strategies. Assessment projects, no matter how sophisticated or simplistic, are encouraged and performed throughout the department (M. Radkiewicz, personal communication, Mar. 29, 2007). EMSA leadership encourages departments to phase out assessment methods that are outdated or deemed ineffective. The leadership also encourages departments to continue long-running assessment efforts.

Student Affairs' major point of collaboration with Academic Affairs occurs with the Office of Academic Assessment. This office seeks to support quality student learning and foster excellence in educational practices by establishing and maintaining a culture of assessment and improvement at the course, program, and institution levels ("Assessment Headquarters," n.d.). The assessment coordinator has many interactions with this office, where each offers data and suggestions. In addition to the connection to the Office of Academic Assessment, Student Affairs also draws on faculty expertise for projects. The Office of Undergraduate Studies currently plans to add an internal academic assessment coordinator position that would provide a more direct liaison to the assessment coordinator in EMSA (K. Pugliesi, personal communication, Apr. 4, 2007).

Current students are also involved in the assessment process at NAU. EMSA takes great pride in supporting their educational endeavors by offering graduate assistantships in assessment. Doing so helps the division by having two dedicated student employees whose main job responsibilities are assessment tasks. The graduate assistants have skill sets, like the assessment coordinator, to help guide employees of the division in determining and implementing assessment projects. In addition to the two graduate assistants, student leaders have become interested in assessment. One student organization that has initiated assessment projects is the Associated Students of Northern Arizona University (ASNAU). This organization serves the university as a representative student voice at the campus, local, state, and national levels ("Associated Students," n.d.). ASNAU initiated a survey of students' opinions about implementing a new student activity fee and consulted the assessment coordinator regarding its administration. ASNAU members used the survey results to gauge support for the fee, which was seen as favorable and was implemented the subsequent year.

Example of Assessment and How Results Are Used

Although there have been many successful assessment projects at Northern Arizona University, the annual Assessment Fair has been an integral part of linking faculty, staff, and students together in the assessment process. The current assessment coordinator developed the idea of an Assessment Fair five years ago. It has developed into a campuswide activity where faculty, staff, and students from departments throughout the university meet to learn about the results of individual and departmental assessment efforts aimed at improving student success at Northern Arizona University. The Assessment Fair is an opportunity to build connections in the NAU community. It is a time to see what others are doing, share accomplishments, and think critically about programs and services. This event showcases how assessment is being used across campus to improve student learning, gauge student satisfaction, evaluate student services, and otherwise contribute to work at the university ("Fifth Annual," 2007).

NEW DIRECTIONS FOR STUDENT SERVICES • DOI: 10.1002/ss

Faculty, staff, students, and Flagstaff community members display posters of their assessment projects, including the findings of student satisfaction surveys, retention studies, student learning outcomes, and other such activities. Saltonstall states, "This is a chance to recognize the efforts of those who conduct assessment above and beyond all their other job responsibilities. Presenters will demonstrate the usefulness of assessment to the varied work of the University, helping us all better understand whether we are achieving our institutional, departmental and program goals" ("Fair to Showcase," 2006, p. 1). Rebecca Cole feels that the Assessment Fair is a "phenomenal" event because of the high faculty turnout (personal communication, Mar. 28, 2007).

The Assessment Fair allows all departments and organizations on campus, including faculty, staff, and students along with community members, to display their assessment results. The beauty of the Assessment Fair is that it allows departments to showcase their assessments while networking with others who conduct assessment on campus. The Assessment Fair holds a postevent activity where posters are displayed in various academic and EMSA offices to share information to those who may not have attended the Assessment Fair.

Tips for Implementing the Process

For those considering reviewing their assessment program or creating one for the first time, we point out that it is important to develop a networking and team-oriented approach to assessment. Support and guidance from leadership are important in initiating the process, but garnering support from individual departments is instrumental to making the assessment process sustainable. It is also essential to combine assessment and strategic planning from the beginning in order to develop assessment goals that align with divisional and university goals. These goals will serve as markers and guideposts when developing assessment priorities. Relying on frameworks and demonstrated models and standards is important. In tandem with the reliance on the assessment literature, including Upcraft and Schuh (1996), EMSA also uses standards from the Council for the Advancement of Standards (CAS) as a reference for the assessment process. CAS delivers the *Book of Professional Standards for Higher Education* (2006), which is designed to lead to a host of quality-controlled programs and services ("Twenty Five," 2006).

It is vital to show that assessment is encouraged within Student Affairs because it will help the culture of assessment to develop. Additionally, we must foster opportunities for individuals and departments to participate in research and assessment so that colleagues and supervisors encourage assessment. Moreover, a culture of assessment can be nurtured in the division by introducing all new employees to the assessment process. Developing the assessment coordinator position helps especially to bring the mission, goals, and values of assessment together. It is absolutely critical to have the right person in the coordinator position, someone who can relate to people both within and outside the division. This person must be adept at cultivating relationships and creating an investment in the assessment process by other stakeholders.

Overcoming Barriers to Assessing Student Learning and Development

There have been challenges with the implementation of a comprehensive assessment program at NAU. Initially, there was a sense of anxiety among the staff concerning assessment. Employees were concerned about their programs and even their job security if assessment results were negative. For other staff lacking confidence and competence, the challenge of learning to perform assessment properly created anxiety. Erwin (1991) believes that Student Affairs staff may feel threatened by assessment and react with fear— and occasionally hostility. To alleviate the fear and anxiety, it was important to articulate to staff within the division that the purpose of assessment was to improve effective service to NAU's students by judging the performance of the program, not individual staff members. It was and continues to be important to have staff feel comfortable reporting statistics and outcomes even if there are some unfavorable results. When departments develop assessment reports, this allows upper leadership to allocate additional resources to those particular programs that are effective. Anytime assessment is performed, regardless if it shows positive or challenging results for the department, it opens new opportunities to reexamine and redefine current approaches to make them more effective.

With a comprehensive assessment program that is supported by leadership; involves students, staff, and faculty; and includes an assessment coordinator position, a culture of assessment and student learning can be embedded within a division, leading to increased program effectiveness. It will also promote opportunities for employees and leadership to continuously evaluate programs and services provided by Student Affairs departments. All this will show the ultimate reason assessment is performed: to ensure student success.

References

"Assessment Headquarters." n.d. Retrieved Mar. 29, 2007, from http://www4.nau.edu/assessment/.

"Associated Students." n.d. Retrieved Mar. 29, 2007, from http://home.nau.edu/asnau/.

Council for the Advancement of Standards in Higher Education (CAS). *The Book of Professional Standards for Higher Education.* Washington, D.C.: CAS, 2006.

Erwin, T. D. *Assessing Student Learning and Development.* San Francisco: Jossey-Bass, 1991.

"Fair to Showcase." 2006. Retrieved Mar. 29, 2007, from http://www4.nau.edu/insidenau/bumps/2006/3_15_06/assessment.htm.

"Fifth Annual Assessment Fair." 2007. Retrieved Oct. 15, 2007, from http://home.nau.edu/%5Cassessment%5Cfair2007.asp.

Saltonstall, M. "Offices of Assessment in Student Affairs: Permanent Fixtures, Temporary Expertise, or Passing Fancy?" *National Association of Student Personnel Administrators Net RESULTS E-Zine*, 2006.

"Self-Study Report Draft." 2007. Retrieved Apr. 1, 2007, from http://jan.ucc.nau.edu/~nca-p/report/nca-ss-report-draft-20070202.pdf.

"Top 100." 2006. Retrieved Mar. 29, 2007, from http://www.hispanicoutlook.com/top100.htm.

"Twenty-Five Years of Professional Services." 2006. Retrieved Apr. 18, 2007, from http://www.cas.edu/.

Upcraft, M. L., and Schuh, J. H. *Assessment in Student Affairs: A Guide for Practitioners.* San Francisco: Jossey-Bass, 1996.

MICHAEL F. BUTCHER is coordinator of operations at the Office of Residence Life at Northern Arizona University (NAU).

MARGOT SALTONSTALL is the assessment coordinator for the Division of Enrollment Management and Student Affairs at NAU.

SARAH BICKEL is associate vice president for student affairs at NAU.

RICK BRANDEL is the dean of students at NAU.

NEW DIRECTIONS FOR STUDENT SERVICES • DOI: 10.1002/ss

7

This chapter provides a glimpse of student affairs assessment at North Carolina State University including a specific example of assessment, tips to implementing assessment at your institution, and barriers encountered when implementing the process at North Carolina State University.

North Carolina State University

Carrie L. Zelna

Overview of Institutional Culture

North Carolina State University is a research extensive university located in the state's capital in the well-known Research Triangle Park. Founded in 1887, this land-grant institution spans 2,110 acres on the Raleigh campus, plus more than 101,000 acres in research and extension farms, forests, and facilities throughout the state. NC State has a student population of more than thirty-one thousand students from nearly one hundred countries pursuing baccalaureate degrees in 103 fields, master's degrees in 110 fields, doctoral degrees in 61 fields, and a doctorate of veterinary medicine.

NC State is a national leader in the STEM disciplines (science, technology, engineering, and math), with comparable strengths in agriculture, humanities, and social sciences. According to our mission statement, NC State provides leadership for intellectual, cultural, social, economic, and technological development within the state, the nation, and the world.

Division of Student Affairs at NC State University

NC State is divided into ten colleges and six administrative divisions, including the Division of Student Affairs. The chief student affairs officer, the vice chancellor for student affairs, reports to the chancellor and serves on the chancellor's executive team. The motto in the Division of Student Affairs, "Students First," has influenced the university's administrative leadership team. The mission of the Division of Student Affairs is to offer programs and

NEW DIRECTIONS FOR STUDENT SERVICES, no. 127, Fall 2009 © Wiley Periodicals, Inc.
Published online in Wiley InterScience (www.interscience.wiley.com) • DOI: 10.1002/ss.328

services for students and the larger community to enhance quality of life; facilitate intellectual, ethical, and personal growth; and create a culture that engenders respect for human diversity. To fulfill our mission and have the greatest impact on student learning and success, the division employs more than six hundred employees in thirty-five departments. The division is made up of three types of units: those traditionally housed in student affairs, such as dining, housing, counseling, and campus activities; programs not traditionally housed in student affairs such as the visual and performing arts; and departments that teach academic classes such as ROTC, physical education, and music.

Overview of the Assessment Process

Assessment of outcomes in Student Affairs is a process that has evolved a great deal over the course of the past several years. Although having a mission, objectives, and outcomes for each of the thirty-five units has been an expectation since 2003, it was not until the shift in focus from "assessment of outcomes" to "planning" that division staff fully understood the connection between assessment and data-driven decision making. Finding the process that worked best for the division was not without difficulty, but Student Affairs is now on the right path.

The Student Affairs Research and Assessment (SARA) office facilitates outcomes-based planning and assessment in Student Affairs at NC State. The SARA office provides support to the division's units by offering assistance with writing objectives and outcomes, navigating planning processes, designing studies, completing Human Subjects paperwork, sampling, supporting quantitative and qualitative methods, analyzing data, and supporting evidence-based decision making. Assistance is delivered through a variety of modes, including individual one-on-one meetings, attendance at unit staff meetings, email, and phone consultation. Depending on the background and comfort level of the staff involved, some units request one contact on a project and at other times SARA works with a unit for the duration of the study.

Present Process. On the basis of the mission and structure of the Division of Student Affairs, the staff spends a great deal of time programming. As a result, project planning is an area where most of the staff excel. Shifting from an assessment-driven process to a department-level planning process was a better fit for the organization. The staff tended to be much more excited about considering how they teach to their outcomes rather than first thinking about "assessment." Once they had an opportunity to review all their significant activities and how those activities map to their department-level learning outcomes, they were better able to effectively and efficiently consider assessment.

The quality of the department-level learning outcomes has increased with the new planning process. The staff have been better able to articulate learning outcomes as a result of tying their significant activities back to department-level outcomes. This process has helped the staff to identify missing outcomes or significant activities that are not directly tied to unit outcomes. In addition, they can more clearly identify where they are spending their resources, including staff time and money. Responsibility for the planning and assessment of the departments is at the director level, but in most units multiple levels of staff are involved with all of the assessment components, such as articulation of objectives and outcomes, study design, creation of instruments, analysis of data, decision making, and implementation of decisions.

The SARA office facilitates Student Affairs Assessment Team (SAAT), which comprises ten division members. These members represent the assistant and associate vice chancellors in the division, and the units for which these senior leaders are responsible. In addition, there are two division faculty members and one graduate student on the team. The diversity of SAAT, in terms of size and scope of the units represented, offers excellent opportunities for valuable discussion on the role of assessment in the Division of Student Affairs, as well as reasonable expectations for unit-level assessment activities and reports. In addition to setting timelines and requirements for assessment for the division, SAAT is responsible for creating guidelines for reports, determining criteria for review of the reports, reviewing unit reports, and giving written feedback to the units.

Assessment Reports. Every summer, the units are required to write a report in order to ensure that assessment is occurring systematically across the division. The reports are intended to be snapshots of assessment, and they serve as vessels to capture the spirit of the assessment process. Providing data on every assessment effort in every unit would create cumbersome reports; therefore units are asked to report on their assessment of only two outcomes per year. Limiting the report to two outcomes makes the reporting process much more manageable.

Example of Assessment and How Results Are Used

The Office of Student Conduct (OSC) at NC State has engaged in assessment for more than six years. Early in the process, the staff attempted to review not only satisfaction with services but also the impact of various sanctions such as parental notification. These attempts required students found guilty of a violation to respond to a questionnaire; as one might expect, the return rate was low. The data were not useful, so the staff continued to look for different ways to assess their work.

OSC continued to refine learning outcomes over the years, and as the office staff did so, new and better ways of measuring impact were identified. The department now has a comprehensive set of outcomes, but this example will focus on the assessment of one of the Office of Student Conduct's learning outcomes and how results were used to improve the work of this important office. What follows is a brief summary of the assessment of one specific learning outcome.

Outcome: Students who violate the code will demonstrate insight into how their behavior affects all aspects of their life.

Background: When a student is accused of a significant violation of the Code of Student Conduct, the student is required to meet with the Office of Student Conduct. Students are interviewed by a staff member and are asked a series of questions regarding the incident. If they are found guilty or admit guilt, then the staff member engages the student in a conversation about the incident and other related personal issues such as progress in school and relationships. The student is then required to write a reflection paper. There are eleven standard questions that every student must answer, plus additional questions for some specific cases.

Methodology: A total of 259 students who were found guilty of a violation of the code were assigned a paper with questions specifically written to correspond with the criteria for development of insight and impact on life issues, as identified in the learning outcome. A rubric was used to review the papers. The rubric was created based on a theory of insight by Mary M. Murray (1995). In her book *Artwork of the Mind*, Murray describes how to determine the development of insight through writing. Initially twenty papers were drawn randomly to test the rubric. The rubric originally had a scale with three categories—beginning, developing, and achieved—and six dimensions based on the theory and practice. In total, twenty-two papers were drawn and reviewed according to the rubric.

Findings: The data gathered were reviewed in the aggregate by dimension. As mentioned previously, the rubric was based on the insight theory by Murray (1995), so the analysis centered on the constructs for which the students had and had not shown achievement. The weakest areas for the group were self-perception and application. Most of the students reached the "achieved" category in the dimensions of separation/objectivity and dissonance. Overall, the dimension understanding/change in perspective was lower and self-perception and resolution both had the majority in the "developing" category. These findings were then used to make changes to how the unit worked with individual students as well as how they assessed some of the dimensions.

One significant change that was expected to have an impact on development was the reordering and changes to the layout of the reflection questions. The analysis indicated that students were not processing the impact on others outside of the situation as expected, so the questions were reordered and the layout changed to make that aspect of the paper more prominent. The staff was also asked to focus on this area more intentionally in conversations with students.

In addition to these changes, the rubric was expanded from a scale of three to four, and the dimensions were expanded from six to seven to allow more detail in assessment of the reflection. It was clear that the category "developing" needed to be delineated into two categories to better demonstrate the level of development of insight.

Tips for Implementing the Process

The culture of the division and institution has a tremendous impact on success of implementation. Steps to take to institutionalize assessment in student affairs at your institution may include reviewing models from other institutions, choosing a model that appears to fit well with the culture in your division and at your institution, and modifying the model as necessary to ensure success. For those who are just starting the process of implementing assessment, we offer some lessons we have learned from our experience to facilitate your process:

Hire an assessment professional. Whether you hire a professional solely for student affairs or arrange for help through the institutional research office on your campus, it is critical to have someone who is focused on assessment in student affairs.

Maintain a positive attitude. It is not what you say; it is how you say it. It is true that positive attitudes are contagious.

Encourage excellence. The assessment process is not simply for accreditation (although that is also a reality). Sometimes people need to know there is a "requirement" to be motivated, but most people in student affairs respond best to the notion of making sure that students are learning what you want them to learn. Student affairs staff take pride in their work and want it to be the best it can be so be sure to demonstrate for them how the assessment process can help them enhance their program.

Require a comprehensive set of objectives and outcomes. Implementing a planning process requires a comprehensive set of objectives and outcomes for each unit. The objectives and outcomes then frame the planning and assessment process.

Engage in planning. Planning is really step one. It is common to start with assessment and then move on to the topic of activities or initiatives. In reality, outcomes are all about what you want students to learn. The outcomes are not about measurement. The first question after "What do you want them to learn?" should be "How are you going to teach them?" Measurement of learning comes after thoughtful consideration of how you teach. The data then enable enhancement or change.

Make the link back to the university clear. Include an exercise in linking unit-level outcomes back to the division and university mission. This will underscore the contribution their unit makes to the institution and may even help units articulate the connection for others on campus.

Use a team. Having an assessment team improves communication with the division, facilitates buy-in, and is simply a lot of fun. The purpose of the group may morph over time as your process grows. The team may serve as a review group for reports or an advisory group for your assessment professional.

Involve all levels of staff. Everyone should be involved with assessment, including senior student affairs administrators.

Communicate how the document will be used at all levels. Some areas might be concerned about who will see the assessment reports; others want to know that someone will see the information and respond to it in a timely manner. If there are other uses for the reports, be sure to let them know. Even though the document might be "public information," it is best to be up front with them about how student affairs will use the information.

Keep reports as simple as possible. Many reporting processes require a lot of information, and reports end up being much longer than needed. If the process is indeed for the benefit of the unit, then ask only for what is necessary to demonstrate that assessment is systematic and data are used to make decisions.

Provide appropriate structure. Many student affairs staff are somewhat intimidated by the assessment process. Imposing structure does not reduce buy-in; it reduces anxiety. Once they feel comfortable with assessment, they will be more invested and will be better able to see the benefits for their unit.

Be flexible. Do not be afraid to make changes throughout the process, and embrace creative ideas and strategies. People like to see that you are responsive to their needs.

Overcoming Barriers to Assessing Student Learning and Development

Although there are a number of barriers any time you begin a new process, the biggest one for our process was a lack of expertise in data analysis at the unit level. When the assessment process was first implemented, the intention was for all units to complete data analysis at the unit level. We have stuck to that strategy wherever possible, meaning when a staff member in that unit has the necessary expertise. However, data analysis really became an issue as we were telling staff who had no training that they had to complete their own analysis. The next strategy we tried was to train these staff members, but that was not an efficient or effective solution. Asking them to learn how to analyze data, specifically survey data, increased their stress level and required funding. In cases where we were able to find a staff member willing to learn, and able to pay for the training, the person used the skill only once or twice a year at most and often forgot what was learned.

As a short-term solution, the director of the Student Affairs Assessment Office is taking on data analysis case by case. In addition, SARA has also taken on interns from the Adult and Higher Education department to reduce some of the workload for the director so that she can spend more time on data analysis. This interim strategy seems to be working well. However, a long-term solution, which is still in the planning stages, is to hire an assistant director for SARA in order to further enhance support provided to the Division of Student Affairs in the assessment of their services and programs.

Reference

Murray, M. M. *Artwork of the Mind*. Cresskill, N.J.: Hampton Press, 1995.

CARRIE L. ZELNA is the director of student affairs research and assessment at North Carolina State University.

8

This chapter provides a glimpse of student affairs assessment at Oregon State University including a specific example of assessment, tips to implementing assessment at your institution, and barriers encountered when implementing the process at Oregon State University.

Oregon State University

Rebecca A. Sanderson, Patricia L. Ketcham

Overview of Institutional Culture

Oregon State University (OSU) is located in Corvallis, a community of fifty-three thousand people situated in the heart of the Willamette Valley between Portland and Eugene. Approximately 15,700 undergraduate and 3,400 graduate students, including 2,600 U.S. students of color and 950 international students, are currently enrolled at OSU across eleven academic colleges. OSU programs in engineering, environmental sciences, forestry, pharmacy, and a variety of other programs are nationally recognized for their high quality.

Within the organizational structure of the university, the vice provost for student affairs reports directly to the provost and executive vice president. Currently, the Division of Student Affairs comprises fourteen departments and offices. The division imparts the essential leadership for the out-of-classroom education of students, the co-curriculum that complements and supplements the academic areas, and the various services necessary for successful student retention and graduation. As a division, Student Affairs has positioned itself "to be learners and leaders in a dynamic educational and social environment. We [the division] choose to empower students to pursue their best possible futures and to contribute to Oregon State University in a way that supports achievement of its desired outcomes" ("This Is Our Anthem," 2006, p. 6).

NEW DIRECTIONS FOR STUDENT SERVICES, no. 127, Fall 2009 © Wiley Periodicals, Inc.
Published online in Wiley InterScience (www.interscience.wiley.com) • DOI: 10.1002/ss.329

Overview of the Division of Student Affairs

The mission of the Division of Student Affairs is to contribute to and facilitate the success of students and Oregon State University. Central to the mission is the vision of Student Affairs that is guided by three tenets for faculty and staff:

- Provide leadership for the positive development of community at Oregon State University.
- Collaborate with others to enhance the educational environment and support the teaching and learning process.
- Value and respect the individual and believe that sharing knowledge changes lives ["This Is Our Anthem," 2006, p. 2].

"Oregon State University's primary responsibility to students is to promote student success, defined as the degree to which students achieve their goals" ("This Is Our Anthem," 2006, p. 8). No other outcome is more important. OSU students can expect a Student Affairs Division that is committed to organizing "educational structures, activities, programs, services and relationships in a dynamic environment for a diverse population in such a way as to expand and elevate student aspirations and visions of what constitutes success" ("This Is Our Anthem," 2006, p. 8). The primary goal of organizing opportunities in such a manner is to give students possibilities for engagement in a variety of programs and services that enhance communication, promote active citizenship, foster a healthy lifestyle, develop interpersonal and intrapersonal competence, exercise critical thinking and analytical skills, and maintain a lifelong interest in learning. The philosophy of Student Affairs is firmly grounded in the belief that an engaged student is far more likely to achieve and be successful than a disengaged student.

Overview of the Assessment Process

The Division of Student Affairs began work assessing programs, services, and student learning nearly a decade ago as an outgrowth of the division-wide planning process mentioned previously. Assessment and the development of an Assessment Council was one initiative that grew from this planning process. Initially, the council was charged with leading the assessment efforts and developing a structure to support the assessment work. Two guiding principles permeated the work and continue to sustain the effort. First, assessment is based in learning and thus is a learning activity. Second, the overarching goal of assessment is improvement in programs and services, and ultimately in student learning.

An Assessment Council comprising volunteers from many departments in student affairs began the work of educating themselves and then educating others about assessment. The key functions of the council are:

- Educating the membership of the Assessment Council and others through professional development activities
- Managing anxiety engendered by the expectation that assessment was a required part of every department or program
- Setting standards for assessment
- Serving as consultants to departments
- Assessing the influence of their efforts on development of an assessment culture in the division

The leadership role of the Assessment Council continues today, and the membership includes academic colleagues as well as student affairs colleagues. The charge for the current Assessment Council makes clear the responsibilities of the council and also promotes flexibility as needs change and expertise increases. The key to assessing student learning has been the supportive and educative role of the Assessment Council. It has enabled departments to understand the role of assessment of student learning, as well as collaborate and share knowledge, ideas, and frustrations. Several specific strategies have been used in order to increase knowledge and application of good assessment practices. They have primarily fallen into four categories:

1. Shared readings from books and articles
2. Workshops and symposia
3. Consultations with experts in the field
4. Peer review of departmental and unit assessment plans

Currently, the Assessment Council is also responsible for setting the structure, format, submission timelines, and review process for assessment plans and reports that are required of every department and unit within the division, including the Office of the Vice Provost. Plans and reports are submitted annually and are reviewed by the membership of the Assessment Council. Council members then meet with departments and provide feedback concerning the student learning dimensions of the plans and reports. Specific information about the process, the expectations, and the review process is posted on the Student Affairs Research and Evaluation (SARE) webpage.

Responsibility for Assessment and Evaluation. Assessment of student development and learning within the division is the responsibility of the director of SARE, the Assessment Council, and the departments and units within the division. Every department and unit must submit an assessment plan and a follow-up report each year. The Assessment Council reviews these plans and reports and assists departments in improving or better using the information they collect. This structure has worked well for the division; it allows departments and units to set their own assessment cycle in order to fit their regular planning activities and work flow, yet it maintains a standard reporting structure that yields a snapshot regarding all

NEW DIRECTIONS FOR STUDENT SERVICES • DOI: 10.1002/ss

the activities and results of those assessment activities. Departments and units are also responsible for communicating their information to department and unit personnel and other constituencies as appropriate.

Each department and unit has been charged by the Council with developing a structure that will support student learning assessment. Some departments and units developed assessment teams or committees; others use all members of their staff as an assessment team, and still others have appointed an assessment lead person to coordinate the activities of their unit or department. The specific unit or departmental structure for supporting this initiative has been left to the discretion of the department or unit in order to allow flexibility and honor the various departmental and unit cultures as to how work is accomplished.

The Assessment Council has set up a process with specific expectations for the format of reporting assessment plans and reports; however, the learning outcomes that are assessed are based on the particular needs and programs of the unit or department. Although the council has implemented a core set of learning areas for departments to consider in developing their curriculum, the specific learning outcomes are determined at the departmental or unit level. The language and framework for assessment within the division has been standardized to achieve a common language and common expectations for the elements that need to be present. Specific elements of the plan and follow-up report are required of each unit and department. These include mission, goals, learning outcomes, assessment methodologies, implementation plans, results, and decisions and recommendations.

Collaboration with Academic Affairs and Instructional Services. Collaboration within the Division of Student Affairs is fairly well developed in many areas, including assessment. However, collaboration between student affairs and academic areas related to student learning has proved to be more difficult overall. One of the barriers to this collaboration is the difference in expectations for and practices of collaborative educational processes for academic departments and programs. A second barrier is the long-time belief that student learning is the domain of the teaching faculty and does not include student affairs per se. A third barrier is the accreditation process for some academic units (such as business, engineering), which is driven by multiple accrediting bodies with differing expectations. However, Student Affairs is well respected and valued by academic colleagues for the services and programs that are provided. A fourth barrier to maximizing collaboration is the shift within student affairs departments to thinking about services and programs in terms of delivery of curriculum directed toward student learning. Although as a profession Student Affairs has long believed in the educative nature of the co-curriculum, crossover and integration into the academic curriculum (curriculum developed by the professorate) has been difficult to attain.

NEW DIRECTIONS FOR STUDENT SERVICES • DOI: 10.1002/ss

Nevertheless, some inroads have occurred. Specifically, there has been a tremendous collaboration between the Colleges of Business and Engineering and the University Housing and Dining Services (UHDS) with regard to a living and learning community entitled the Austin Entrepreneurship Program. The curricular development, training of resident assistants, and assessment of student learning were collaborative efforts between UHDS and the college faculty representatives.

Student Involvement. Students are primarily the subject of the assessment efforts in Student Affairs. Some efforts to involve students in "making meaning" of assessment results have been successful. Others have asked students what they wanted to learn from particular experiences, employment, or leadership positions and then worked with the students to design experiences to deliver those outcomes. Some have made it a point to transmit the results of their assessments to students, while others have used assessment results as talking points when engaging with students about services or programs.

Example of Assessment and How Results Are Used

One of the key functions of the Student Involvement (SI) program is to encourage and support development of students through participation in clubs and organizations. One mechanism by which this is accomplished is to use student peer advisors to mentor and assist organizations to develop. These student peer advisors—BRIDGES staff (Building Respected, Inclusive, Diverse Groups Educating Students)—support fellow students by serving as a liaison between Student Involvement and the student organization; attending student organization meetings; coaching on organization development, leadership development, event planning, policies, and procedures; and connecting with appropriate resources.

To maximize the effectiveness of the BRIDGES staff, they undergo extensive training and mentoring by the professional staff. During the 2005–06 academic year, the SI professional staff focused on assessing the effectiveness of the training and mentoring of the BRIDGES staff as well as on assessing the ongoing needs of the organizations they serve.

Here is a summary of the outcomes and ways in which assessment information was used by the SI professional and student staff. The SI staff focused on these outcomes in their assessment:

1. BRIDGES staff will be able to practice proper event planning procedures and will be able to teach them to their assigned student organizations.
2. BRIDGES staff will be able to articulate and accurately apply policies and procedures related to student organizations.
3. BRIDGES staff will be able to plan their time in such a way that they meet project timelines.

NEW DIRECTIONS FOR STUDENT SERVICES • DOI: 10.1002/ss

4. BRIDGES staff will be able to analyze needs of their assigned student organizations in order to constructively advise and coach them.
5. SI will determine what student organizations need and want from the SI staff in terms of training and support on topics of leadership development and event planning.

Results from assessment of these outcomes led the SI staff to take these actions:

1. Revamped the delivery system, curriculum, and assignments for BRIDGES student staff training.

    - Created a peer advisor training course (CSSA 406) that all BRIDGES staff (new and returning) participated in.
    - Explanation of BRIDGES student roles and responsibilities was developed with the input and feedback from students. Shared with organizations to clarify expectations and provide guidance to organizations.
    - For staff training, instituted daily Recap Assessment Questions, which were used to make training adjustments along the way.
    - BRIDGES student staff led and presented training sessions for one another in order to increase BRIDGES students' knowledge and confidence for eventually working with organizations.

2. Restructured the BRIDGES student staff team into two teams: Event Specialists and Leadership Development Teams.
3. Event specialists developed workshops to be given multiple times during the year for organizations.
4. Event specialists developed an online event-planning manual for use by organizations.
5. Leadership Development Team created workshops based on feedback from organizations and presented them several times per year.

The particular value of assessment for this organization has been to help them focus on assessing those areas that are of high importance. As the professional and student staff have engaged in intentional conversations as part of the assessment process, it has fostered the kinds of collaborations and focus they have sought. Their assessment plan for the coming year reflects their learning and also builds on findings from the previous report.

The Office of Student Affairs and Research annually compiles a report (by department and unit) on how assessment information has been used by the department or unit. Copies of these reports are located at http://oregonstate.edu/studentaffairs/assessment/departmental.html.

NEW DIRECTIONS FOR STUDENT SERVICES • DOI: 10.1002/ss

Tips for Implementing the Process

Most of the tips listed here as well as others can be found in any number of resources (Bresciani, 2006; Maki, 2004; Palomba and Banta, 1999). The ones given here are those that the OSU Division of Student Affairs has found most helpful:

Align processes with the leadership culture of the organization. To implement processes that will work and be sustainable, they must be aligned with the leadership culture of the organization. At OSU in the Division of Student Affairs, there is a very strong leadership philosophy and practice. Much of how the assessment process and the review process work is directly linked to the leadership practices in the division.

Educate, educate, educate. The model at OSU works because of a strong belief in and support for educating the division about assessment and data-based decision making. If education is transformative, then it must be part of the mix when implementing an assessment program.

Have clear support from the leadership. The vice provost for student affairs at OSU has been very clear in terms of the expectations, leadership, and value of the assessment processes within the division. Further, financial support for education and other projects emanating from the Assessment Council is evident.

Focus efforts on the willing. At OSU the focus has been on the willing, those who had interest and willingness to learn and invest in a process. As a result, energy was conserved and directed into developing positive efforts instead of battling negativity. The result of this practice has been that the nay-saying group has substantially diminished and the focus is now on "How do we do this?" rather than "Do we have to do this?"

Reflect often. The Assessment Council and the director of SARE consistently reflect on and evaluate the effectiveness of major projects or actions.

Find joy in assessment, and celebrate successes. This tip may seem surprising. However, it has helped to sustain the assessment efforts, particularly when the hurdles seemed overwhelming. Members of the Assessment Council at OSU have found ways in which to feel joy in the good humor, engagement, support, and collegiality present in the council.

Develop a support structure. Assessment is by its very nature a process better done by a group than a lone individual. Develop a support structure with a group of people who are willing to work together to develop a process that is focused on the important questions of the division, department, or unit. The diversity of experiences, opinions, and thinking will prove very valuable.

Ask important questions. Focus questions on areas that are core and of value to the division, department, or unit. Then share the information widely and gain input from others in an effort to make meaning of the information and use it for improvements.

Overcoming Barriers to Assessing Student Learning and Development

There are many barriers to assessing student learning. A common one that has occurred in all departments within the division is in regard to helping Student Affairs faculty and staff understand and be able to write meaningful learning outcomes. Many people in the division do not have a background in pedagogy and thus are unaccustomed to thinking in terms of learning outcomes. As an example of a departmental assessment council that worked to overcome this barrier to units, the Recreational Sports Assessment Council developed a training experience and opportunities to practice developing meaningful learning outcomes in program-specific areas. Through their efforts, many other Student Affairs departments are using their format and process to help their faculty and staff better understand, develop, write, and measure learning outcomes.

References

Bresciani, M. J. *Outcomes-based Academic and Co-curricular Program Review: A Compilation of Institutional Good Practices*. Sterling, Va.: Stylus, 2006.

Maki, P. L. *Assessing for Learning*. Sterling, Va.: Stylus, 2004.

Palomba, C. A., and Banta, T. W. *Assessment Essentials: Planning, Implementing, and Improving Assessment in Higher Education*. San Francisco: Jossey-Bass, 1999.

"This Is Our Anthem." [Brochure.] Corvallis: Office of the Vice Provost for Student Affairs, Oregon State University, 2006.

REBECCA A. SANDERSON *is the director of student affairs research and evaluation at Oregon State University.*

PATRICIA L. KETCHAM *is the associate director of health promotion in student health services at Oregon State University.*

9

This chapter provides a glimpse of student affairs assessment at Paradise Valley Community College including a specific example of assessment, tips to implementing assessment at your institution, and barriers encountered when implementing the process at Paradise Valley Community College.

Paradise Valley Community College

Paul A. Dale

Overview of Institutional Culture

Paradise Valley Community College (PVCC), located in Phoenix, Arizona, is part of the Maricopa County Community College District (MCCCD). There are a total of ten colleges in the MCCCD serving 222,174 credit students annually. PVCC was founded in 1987 and in the fall of 2007 served 8,739 students in credit courses. Approximately 75 percent of incoming students state that transfer to a four-year university is their primary goal of attendance. The college's service area—one of the fastest-growing areas in metropolitan Phoenix, with an expected population increase over the next ten years to exceed 250,000—includes northeast Phoenix and northern Maricopa County and currently serves approximately 500,000 residents.

Since 1997, PVCC has been on a quest to become a "more learning centered" college, as illustrated by Barr and Tagg (1995) and O'Banion (1997). As a result of placing student learning at the core of everything we do, a number of organizational changes were made. First, PVCC's core operating practices are now driven by twelve learning-centered indicators. The first three indicators focus specifically on student learning and assessment:

1. Learning outcomes have been identified and made explicit.
2. Learning outcomes serve as the centerpiece for program and curriculum development.
3. Learning outcomes are measured for the purposes of intervention, remediation, and continuous improvement.

New Directions for Student Services, no. 127, Fall 2009 © Wiley Periodicals, Inc.
Published online in Wiley InterScience (www.interscience.wiley.com) • DOI: 10.1002/ss.330

Second, PVCC reorganized its organizational structure to better align resources with student learning and better support the comprehensive student learning experience that recognizes and values learning in and out of the classroom. There are three organizational divisions: Learning (formerly academic affairs), Learning Support Services (formerly student affairs), and Administrative Services. The Learning Support Services division melds the traditional student affairs functions with all of the out-of-class academic support units in an effort to link the in-class and out-of-class learning experience for students. Third, the Learning Support Services division committed to identifying and making concrete learning outcomes, assessing learning outcomes in order to improve learning and service productivity, and aligning student affairs policies and procedures to maximize student learning (Dale, 2003).

Overview of the Division of Student Affairs/Services

The Learning Support Services division has three primary clusters: Student Development (Student Life and Leadership, Service Learning, Academic Advising, Athletics, Disability Services, Counseling, Learning Support Center, New Student Programs), Student Services (Admissions and Records, Financial Aid, Testing, Child Development Center), and Learning Technologies (Computer Commons, Instructional Technology, Infrastructure Technologies, Media, Center for Distance Learning). The mission of the Learning Support Services Division is to create conditions that motivate and inspire students to engage in the learning process and educationally purposeful activities, become involved in college and community life, and complete desired educational goals—therefore increasing their quality of life. The division, through service, contributes to students' emotional, recreational, civic, and social development.

Student learning and success outcomes are placed at the center of the "mental model" that drives the division's operation. This model also guides development of the division's initial assessment strategy and the current annual assessment implementation. Two seminal publications—*The Student Learning Imperative: Implications for Student Affairs* (American College Personnel Association, 1994) and *Powerful Partnerships: A Shared Responsibility for Learning* (American Association for Higher Education, American College Personnel Association, and National Association for Student Personnel Administrators, 1998)—gave inspiration and direction for this transformation into a more learning-centered perspective. The model shows the interrelationship of departments' roles in the student learning process, factors that influence student persistence, and student learning and success outcomes. From the interrelationship of these factors, departmental learning outcomes and goals and objectives are developed. Assessment serves as the feedback loop for the entire operational relationship.

As noted in the model, the Student Learning and Success Outcomes serve as the centerpiece for all activity and represent what students are expected to learn as a result of interacting and engaging with the division's programs and services. Figure 9.1 lists the outcomes. To connect and align the college's general education outcomes with student success outcomes, recently the college assessment committee requested addition of general education outcomes to better align in-class and out-of-class learning outcomes.

The request to integrate the general education outcome language into the overall college student learning and success outcomes is an indicator that faculty see the efficacy of viewing student learning from a holistic point of view. This also supports the expectation that student affairs staff make a contribution to the overall student learning experience at the college. At PVCC, the general education faculty developed learning outcomes and corresponding rubrics. Faculty are also expected, and are welcomed participants, in overall evaluation of the effectiveness of student affairs programs and services. Student affairs assessment reports on the measures of general education learning outcomes are shared with the faculty-led general education assessment committee. Several student affairs programs have faculty as members of advisory committees, and there is faculty representation on the out-of-class assessment committee. Faculty played key roles in evaluating

Figure 9.1. Student Learning and Success Outcomes

I will be successful if I:

- Am able to identify educational, personal, and career goals
- Know how degree and certificate requirements and general education courses assist me in reaching educational goals
- Become an independent, self-sufficient learner through monitoring of my educational, personal, and career goals
- Become an active, engaged learner and critical thinker
- Recognize how to establish effective relationships with other students, faculty, and staff
- Participate in leadership and civic engagement activities
- Demonstrate behavior that respects individual uniqueness and differences
- Engage in wellness activities
- Have gained these life skills:
    - THINK—critically, creatively, and practically
    - COMMUNICATE—through speaking, writing, listening, and reading
    - RESEARCH—find, identify, evaluate, and apply information
    - SOLVE PROBLEMS—identify causes, options, and solutions
    - USE TECHNOLOGY—online, electronic, and multimedia resources

NEW DIRECTIONS FOR STUDENT SERVICES • DOI: 10.1002/ss

the effectiveness of such programs as intercollegiate athletics, service learning, the child development center, and academic advising. Faculty review and provide feedback on the out-of-class assessment plans and reports. In a learning-centered culture, both faculty and administration expect the student affairs units to demonstrate patterns of evidence that students are learning as a result of participating in programs and services.

Overview of the Assessment Process

At PVCC, assessment of student learning outside the classroom has been under way since 2002. Departmental outcomes are aligned with the overall student success and learning outcomes. PVCC's development of outcomes was influenced by Bresciani (2001), who articulated program outcomes as measures of whether or not the task was completed and learning outcomes addressing both cognitive and affective domains.

Initially, each unit identified 8 to 10 learning outcomes. To connect the out-of-class assessment with in-class learning, the departments' learning outcomes were then placed on a matrix and where appropriate aligned with the college's general education learning outcomes. Table 9.1 is a sample of the matrix from one of the Learning Support areas. This sample shows three Office of Financial Aid learning outcomes aligned with selected college general education outcomes.

In 2003, five units piloted assessment of student learning, and beginning in 2004 assessment has been required of all Learning Support Services units. The assessment cycle includes three primary phases: planning, measuring (of at least one learning outcome), and reporting. In August, every unit is required to submit an assessment plan (current PVCC plans can be viewed at http://www.pvc.maricopa.edu/lss/projects.html). The assessment plans are evaluated by the out-of-class assessment committee. Each unit is given a feedback form with constructive comments on the essential elements of the plan. Actual assessment activities take place in fall or spring semesters. Unit assessment reports are due annually on July 1 (a summary of the 2005–06 assessment reports is available at http://www.pvc.maricopa. edu/lss/projects.html). The assessment annual reports are also evaluated by the out-of-class assessment committee through use of an assessment rubric. On the basis of the rubric evaluations, three annual assessment awards are given: the "Assessment Cup" (for the unit with the most outstanding comprehensive assessment activities), the First Runner Up award, and an award for "promising" assessment activities.

The assessment plan includes these elements:

- Area or program to be assessed
- Specific learning outcomes to be measured (including general education outcomes)
- Assessment strategy or methodology

NEW DIRECTIONS FOR STUDENT SERVICES • DOI: 10.1002/ss

Table 9.1. Learning Outcomes and General Education Matrix Example

Learning Area	Communication: Listening	Communication: Reading	Communication: Speaking	Communication: Writing	Information Literacy	Problem Solving	Technology
Financial Aid A student will:							
Demonstrate an understanding of the rules and procedures necessary to apply for financial aid	x			x	x		
Develop a personal money management plan to assess his or her current and future financial needs		x		x	x	x	x
Demonstrate ability to research possible outside educational funding sources		x		x	x		x

NEW DIRECTIONS FOR STUDENT SERVICES • DOI: 10.1002/ss

- Expected learning from this assessment activity
- Samples of assessment instruments

The unit managers work with the college's out-of-class assessment coordinator to develop the plan, identify assessment tools, and create an implementation strategy. Assessment plans are an integral part of the department's operation and required as part of the department's overall operational planning process.

The assessment annual report includes these elements:

- What did the area expect to learn as a result of the assessment activity?
- What were the results, and how will the results be used?
- What are the plans for improvements, enhancements, and changes to help students achieve the learning outcome more efficiently and effectively?
- Samples of assessment tools and completed measurements.

Faculty are involved in assessment of out-of-class learning in several ways: faculty-developed general education rubrics are shared and adapted for division use in measuring out-of-class general education learning, units conducting out-of-class general education learning share findings with appropriate faculty, and faculty serve on the out-of-class assessment committee.

PVCC has inconsistently involved students in the assessment process. At the time of this writing, students are not included in development of specific learning outcomes or processes to measure student learning in the out-of-class environment. This inconsistency was noted during our recent reaffirmation of our accreditation. There are a number of steps we are taking to improve in this area: posting student learning outcomes on unit website; creating posters to place on campus listing student learning and success outcomes, where rubrics are used in assessment providing students an overview of the evaluation criteria; and integrating student learning outcomes into student publications such as the Student Handbook.

Example of Assessment and How Results Are Used

An example from the college's initial assessment pilot is the Learning Support Center (LSC), Writing Center Project. The LSC learning outcomes are aligned with the division student learning outcome of "becoming active and engaged learners." The learning outcomes are designed to measure students' ability to solve learning problems in the context of the tutoring relationship. The LSC problem-solving learning outcomes are also aligned with the college's written communication general education outcomes.

LSC learning problem-solving outcomes: Students will be able to:

- Identify opportunities for improvement.
- Identify strategies for improvement.
- Implement strategies for improvement.

General education written communication dimensions: Students will be able to:

- Communicate in writing ideas in an organized manner using an appropriate rhetorical strategy.
- Communicate in writing ideas logically using appropriate language (word choice, voice, and tone), supporting materials, and transitions that meet the needs of the audience.
- Communicate in writing ideas using appropriate grammar, sentence structure, punctuation, spelling, and format, and within a given word count.

During the pilot process, tutors measured the outcomes for his or her tutoring sessions by observation of the student's ability level to master the LSC problem-solving and written communication general education outcomes. These outcomes were measured in each tutoring session using a 0–3 scale. During the pilot, tutors worked with thirty-six students in 165 tutoring sessions. These students participated in an average of 4.6 sessions. Student scores from only their first and last tutoring sessions were used in the analysis in order to attempt to demonstrate learning over time. Improvement in the aggregate was shown; however, some students' final scores were lower than their initial scores, while some students showed no improvement (net changes not statistically significant).

Tips for Implementing the Process

The most valuable foundation for the assessment initiative at PVCC was establishment of learning as the core organizational value and centerpiece for delivery of student affairs programs and services. The commitment to provide up-front professional development for student affairs professionals to become grounded in the contemporary literature that supports the premise of student learning outside the classroom as a valued part of the students' total college experience was essential. Here are specific tips for implementing an effective assessment program:

- Staff training activities on the mechanics of assessment activities including identification of learning outcomes and measurement best practices.
- Use of structured assessment planning and reporting tools that offer a step-by-step process with criteria outlining key elements is critical for success. Collection and synthesis of all unit plans at the division level is also critical. For the 2006–07 summary of PVCC assessment plans, see http://www.pvc.maricopa.edu/lss/projects.html.
- After several years without any centralized support of assessment, PVCC ultimately secured an out-of-class assessment consultant to work onsite fifteen hours a week to assist with the process. The consultant provided

coaching, training, and professional development events and chaired the out-of-class assessment committee.

Where possible, integrate use of faculty-developed assessment rubrics. There are also several strategies to avoid in implementing an effective assessment initiative.

Bottom-Up Versus Top-Down. At PVCC, initially each unit developed specific learning outcomes essential to student learning realized from provision of programs and services. It was only after unit-level learning outcomes were developed that collegewide out-of-class student success and learning outcomes were developed. The global success and learning outcomes permit greater alignment of common learning outcomes, allow integration of learning outcomes tied to student persistence factors to be incorporated universally across many units, and aid sharing of measurement tools across units. Establishing global learning outcomes first and then writing unit-level learning outcomes creates a more coherent assessment plan.

Too Many Learning Outcomes. Initially each unit wrote 8 to 10 learning outcomes. This is noble, and perhaps the student learning within student affairs units is this comprehensive, but it is not impossible to effectively measure annually more than two or three well-written outcomes. Start small while developing outcomes, and focus on the most seminal student learning that is occurring at the unit level.

Overcoming Barriers to Assessing Student Learning and Development

In times of tight budgets, reduced staffing, and competing program and service priorities, the notion of assessing student learning in the out-of-class environment can be viewed as a nonessential, add-on responsibility. With other competing initiatives such as enrollment management, diversity programming, and underprepared student programming and services, it is easy to realize that addition of a comprehensive assessment program can be a daunting task. There was significant buy-in and ownership of implementing learning-centered practices, but the reality of the complexities and challenges of actual assessment of student learning served to be a problematic barrier.

Ultimately, assessment came to be viewed and accepted by staff as a normal part of the existing organizational systems and an essential everyday lens for viewing delivery of programs and services. Several strategies were used to overcome this barrier:

- Integrate the assessment protocol into the mental model of the student affairs operations. Require that summaries of assessment plans and annual reports become part of the unit annual reporting structure.

- Include assessment activities as part of the unit leaders' annual evaluation process.
- Vigorously celebrate assessment accomplishments. Annual awarding of the Assessment Cup was somewhat skeptically received, but it has proven to be a cherished and sought-after distinction.
- Include assessment issues and discussions of substance on the regular division meeting agendas.
- Create a sense of importance and value of measuring student learning by requiring current and valid assessment as a prerequisite for submitting future budget requests.

References

American Association of Higher Education (AAHE), American College Personnel Association (ACPA), and National Association of Student Personnel Administrators (NASPA). *Powerful Partnerships: A Shared Responsibility for Learning.* Washington, D.C.: AAHE, ACPA, NASPA, 1998.

American College Personnel Association. *The Student Learning Imperative: Implications for Student Affairs.* Washington, D.C.: ACPA, 1994.

Barr, R. B., and Tagg, J. "From Teaching to Learning: A New Paradigm for Undergraduate Education." *Change,* 1995, 27(6), 12–25.

Bresciani, M. J. "Writing Measurable and Meaningful Outcomes." *National Association of Student Personnel Administrators NetResults E-Zine,* 2001. Retrieved Oct. 16, 2007, from www.naspa.org.

Dale, P. "A Journey in Becoming More Learning-centered." *National Association of Student Personnel Administrators NetResults E-Zine,* 2003. Retrieved Nov. 11, 2007, from www.naspa.org.

O'Banion, T. "A Learning College for the 21st Century." American Council on Education/Oryx Press series on Higher Education. Phoenix, Ariz.: Oryx Press, 1997.

PAUL A. DALE serves as vice president of learning support services at Paradise Valley Community College.

NEW DIRECTIONS FOR STUDENT SERVICES • DOI: 10.1002/ss

10

This chapter provides a glimpse of student affairs assessment at the Pennsylvania State University including a specific example of assessment, tips to implementing assessment at your institution, and barriers encountered when implementing the process at the Pennsylvania State University.

The Pennsylvania State University

Philip J. Burlingame, Andrea L. Dowhower

Overview of Institutional Culture

Founded in 1855 as the Farmer's High School, the Pennsylvania State University (Penn State) began as a small college in Centre County providing agricultural education to young men from regional farm families. Penn State became a land-grant university in 1863 following passage of the Morrill Act. Today, Penn State enrolls more than eighty-three thousand students and has more than 420,000 living alumni. Penn State comprises twenty-four campuses, including the University Park campus, which is located adjacent to the Borough of State College in Central Pennsylvania. State College has a population of more than thirty-eight thousand, and the university largely fuels the local economy of the Centre Region.

Overview of the Division of Student Affairs at Penn State

Today, the Division of Student Affairs is headed by a vice president who oversees student affairs operations at the University Park campus as well as nineteen other commonwealth campuses offering undergraduate education. At University Park, the division is made up of seventeen departments employing approximately 350 full-time employees. The Penn State Division of Student Affairs' mission (2005) is to "cultivate student intellectual and personal development by promoting engagement in teaching and learning, academic success, and integration into the Penn State community."

New Directions for Student Services, no. 127, Fall 2009 © Wiley Periodicals, Inc.
Published online in Wiley InterScience (www.interscience.wiley.com) • DOI: 10.1002/ss.331

Researchers have demonstrated that when students are given a structure to help them make meaning and connections out of their in-class and out-of-class educational experiences, a higher level of learning takes place (Cleveland-Innes and Emes, 2005; King, 2007; Reardon, Lumsden, and Meyer, 2005). With this conceptual framework as a backdrop, a new vision for co-curricular learning at Penn State is emerging. Intentional co-curricular learning is now seen as a critical component of the educational experience. Also, it is viewed as an area where students are best served when high expectations for achieving co-curricular learning outcomes are clearly communicated; powerful learning experiences are designed to provoke contemplation and reflection; and reflective writing, meaning making, and evolving self-authorship are encouraged (Ignelzi, 2000; Kegan, 1994; Nash, 2004).

Overview of the Assessment Process

Penn State has a rich tradition of assessment in student affairs. The Student Affairs Research and Assessment (SARA) office evolved from a Residence Life assessment committee and began in the mid-1990s under the leadership of Lee Upcraft and Betty Moore. SARA has grown over time from having one part-time director to having four FTE staff members. The cornerstone of the office's operation has historically been the Penn State Pulse Program, a Gallup-type phone (and Web) surveying process designed to obtain a rapid response from students on various issues, expectations, needs, usage of programs and services, and satisfaction. Thirty students are employed by the program to administer the surveys by phone. These students have become a valuable asset to the program; they offer valuable insights on the survey content and ways to improve the process.

Although the topics for Pulse projects typically come from within Student Affairs on the basis of strategic priorities and initiatives, external units also request Pulse surveys. One of the most prolific users is Penn State's Office of Teaching and Learning with Technology, which has partnered with University Libraries, Information Technology Services, and the Schreyer Institute for Teaching Excellence. In addition, an advisory committee including representatives from undergraduate education; the colleges of engineering, education, and agriculture; the Schreyer Institute for Teaching Excellence; Teaching and Learning with Technology; Institutional Planning and Assessment; and several student affairs units, was formed to extend guidance to the SARA office.

Similar to the shift in the profession and the reorganization within the student affairs division at Penn State, SARA has also experienced a shift in its mission over time. Although understanding the experiences of students through measuring opinions and expectations, tracking use of services and programs, assessing needs, and assessing satisfaction (Upcraft and Schuh, 1996) continue to be important, SARA has recently begun to expand its efforts to assess learning outcomes. The foundation of these efforts is increasing the intentionality of co-curricular programs and services by establishing learning outcomes, communicating these outcomes to students and others, and then assessing the learning.

Concurrent with the work of the Coordinating Committee on University Assessment, student affairs began an initiative to improve its educational programming efforts. For a number of years, Student Affairs has used a systematic way to both track and evaluate the educational programs offered throughout the division. The number of programs as well as the type, attendance, and other basic reporting elements of programming have been reported annually, but the programs have not been critically examined for their effectiveness. With the goal of creating co-curricular certificates, the programming units were asked to complete a cataloguing sheet on each of their "regularly" offered programs. Similar to a conference program proposal, the sheet included an abstract of the program and intended learning outcomes. The certificates, now being piloted, contribute to a more intentional and extended learning experience and a viable means for assessing the intended outcomes. Although some student affairs departments have not yet fully adopted these assessment protocols, they are intended to apply to all educational programming efforts in the division.

Example of Assessment and How Results Are Used

In the mid-1990s, under the leadership of President Graham Spanier, the Penn State Student Newspaper Readership Program began as a pilot program in the residence halls at University Park. Currently, the program, which provides *USA Today*, the *New York Times*, and the local paper to students, is offered on twenty-two of the Penn State campuses. Because of Penn State's success, a similar program is now available at more than five hundred colleges and universities across the country. The goals of the program are to:

- Enhance the learning environment on campus.
- Increase students' knowledge of community, national, and world events.
- Encourage a lifelong daily newspaper readership habit.
- Create more engaged citizens in their local communities (to learn more about the program, visit http://www.newspapers.psu.edu/).

Penn State Pulse has been assessing the effectiveness of the readership program since its inception. Initially, *effectiveness* was defined as use of and satisfaction with the program, use of the newspaper in classes, students' preferred news source, and other evaluative measures. However, the surveys did not measure the impact of newspaper readership on learning. In 2004, Penn State reexamined the goals of the program, and the assessment plan was expanded on the basis of the need to understand the impact the program has on learning outcomes. In partnership with a company called

Educational Benchmarking, SARA revised the existing survey used by Pulse to include more detailed information on students' readership behavior (for example, how frequently they read a paper, how long, and which sections), students' engagement on campus and in the community, and their self-reported gains in various outcomes (such as developing an understanding of current issues, expanding their vocabulary, articulating their views on issues, increasing their reading comprehension).

In the spring of 2005, 1,339 randomly selected University Park students participated in the Student Newspaper Readership Pulse Survey, which had a 27 percent response rate and a ±2.63 margin of error. Although the assessment was conducted on twenty Penn State campuses, this case study will focus only on the findings from University Park. From the survey results, these data speak to use of and satisfaction with the student newspaper readership program:

- Aware of the newspaper readership program: 99 percent
- Read the paper in the last seven days: 83 percent
- Reported spending ten to thirty minutes per day reading the paper: 70 percent
- Had at least one instructor that academic year require them to read a newspaper regularly: 35 percent
- Expressed satisfaction with the program: 86 percent
- Indicated the availability of free newspapers increased their newspaper readership: 91 percent

With the factors seen in Table 10.1, the data were used to assess the relationship between newspaper readership and the intended outcomes by comparing students who read the paper and those who did not, by comparing students who had the paper required in class and those who did not, and by examining the relationship between factors. Overwhelmingly, the evidence suggests a very strong relationship between newspaper readership and outcomes such as developing civic-mindedness and cognitive skills, civic engagement, and being informed and able to articulate views on current issues.

Examination of the effectiveness of use of the newspaper in the classroom compared students who had at least one faculty member require regular newspaper readership and those who did not; it demonstrated a very strong relationship between the intended outcomes and use of the newspaper in class. Arguably, "use in the classroom" mitigates (or controls for) existing differences between students who read a newspaper and those who do not, furnishing greater evidence that readership leads to the intended outcomes of the program (see Table 10.2).

In addition to comparisons based on readership, the analyses included correlations between factors to lend further evidence of the outcomes of newspaper readership. In all cases, the relationships between factors are positive and statistically significant at the 99.9 percent level. Selected findings

New Directions for Student Services • DOI: 10.1002/ss

Table 10.1. Factor Comparisons by Newspaper Readership, with Means

Factors	Did Read	Did Not Read	Significance+
Outcome: informed about social and local issues	3.99	3.36	***
Outcome: informed about national and international issues	3.61	3.13	***
Outcome of newspaper readership: develop civic-mindedness	4.21	3.20	***
Outcome of newspaper readership: develop cognitive skills	3.76	3.01	***
Behavior: classroom and campus engagement	2.86	2.59	**
Behavior: civic engagement	2.28	1.89	***
Outcome from newspaper readership: increased understanding	3.79	3.02	***
Outcome: articulation of views on major issues	4.30	3.75	***

Notes: 7-point scale: 1 = not at all, 4 = moderately, 7 = extremely (or 1 = 0, 2 = 1–2, 3 = 3–4, 4 = 5–6, 5 = 7–8, 6 = 9–10, 7 = more than 10).

+ Significant differences: *** at the .001 level; ** at the .01 level.

from these analyses are in Table 10.3; they demonstrate that readership of local, national, and international news is closely related to students' development of or increase in being informed about national and international

Table 10.2. Factor Comparisons by Classroom Use, with Means

Factors	Used in Class	Not Used in Class	Significance+
Outcome: informed about social and local issues	3.98	3.90	
Outcome: informed about national and international issues	3.69	3.50	*
Outcome of newspaper readership: develop civic-mindedness	4.45	3.94	***
Outcome of newspaper readership: develop cognitive skills	4.10	3.47	***
Behavior: classroom and campus engagement	3.04	2.72	***
Behavior: civic engagement	2.42	2.14	***
Outcome from newspaper readership: increased understanding	4.09	3.52	***
Outcome: articulation of views on major issues	4.40	4.16	**

Notes: 7-point scale: 1 = not at all, 4 = moderately, 7 = extremely (or 1 = 0, 2 = 1–2, 3 = 3–4, 4 = 5–6, 5 = 7–8, 6 = 9–10, 7 = more than 10).

+ Significant differences: *** at the .001 level; ** at the .01 level, * at the .05 level.

**Table 10.3. Relationship to Readership:
Local, National, International News**

Factor	Correlation
Outcome: informed about national and international issues	0.50
Outcome of newspaper readership: develop civic-mindedness	0.53
Outcome of newspaper readership: develop cognitive skills	0.40
Outcome of newspaper readership: increased understanding	0.47
Outcome: articulation of views on major issues	0.37

news, developing civic-mindedness and cognitive skills, understanding issues, and being able to articulate their views on major issues.

These data have been used to support and improve the program in multiple ways. First and foremost, the data strongly support continued use of university resources to fund and staff the program and expand the program to include the Great Valley campus. In addition, the results of this effort are being used to market the program in multiple ways. For example, the program now hires a marketing intern, who has been able to successfully convince first-year seminar faculty to allow her to present information on the program to new students. In addition, the intern has coordinated other marketing strategies such as use of Facebook, sampling efforts, and advertising. Data have also been used to encourage faculty members to use the newspaper in their classes.

Tips for Implementing the Process

An important step when assessing learning is to establish and articulate intended learning outcomes, which are often implicit to student affairs' efforts but not always clearly stated and communicated to others. The process of defining outcomes and determining how to assess those outcomes improves the programs and services offered to students.

Other tips for implementing a plan to assess learning:

- Begin with the literature and the research on what is known about student learning and the outcomes intended by various educational interventions.
- On the basis of the literature, use indirect measures of learning to assess the educational impact of a program. The National Survey of Student Engagement (2006) is a leading example of how to measure the qualities of educational environments that enhance learning.
- Self-reported measures of learning can, under the right circumstances, yield valid data on student learning. Refer to Volkwein's summary (2005) of the literature on self-reported measures.

- Be realistic about the level of learning that can be expected. For example, thinking that one forty-five-minute educational session on alcohol prevention is going to change students' behavior is setting up the program for failure.
- Assess the things most important to the context, including the mission and strategic plan of the institution and the division. Focus on the things that matter most.
- Be aware of the challenges and complexities of measuring outcomes, as summarized by Pascarella and Terenzini (2005). These include their assertions that outcomes are interdependent with learning occurring in multiple settings both in and outside the classroom, that narrowly focusing on any one dimension of learning may limit the understanding, that the magnitude of the change may not be as important as the breadth, and that the timing is important—not only whether an intervention makes a difference but also when.

Overcoming Barriers to Assessing Student Learning and Development

With Penn State's universitywide plan for assessment focusing on student learning, several new challenges emerge for academic leaders charged with developing the university's assessment measures for course-level, program-level, and general education learning outcomes. The first challenge is simply to get faculty to understand the importance of creating an intentional learning environment, creating learning outcomes, and committing to actually assessing student learning. The next challenge is to develop effective strategies to motivate faculty, who see themselves as experts in their content areas, to learn the skills needed to create learning outcomes, understand student learning, and apply appropriate assessment strategies. These same challenges also apply to student affairs educators who are trying to find true measures of student co-curricular learning.

Penn State is a complex organization, and student affairs practitioners often have a difficult time retreating from the demands of their day-to-day work in order to focus on any new or added responsibilities. Under these conditions, it is not easy for practitioners to engage in the scholarly effort required to understand learning theory, write learning outcomes, or evaluate and apply assessment strategies. Still, it is true that much of the educational programming work in student affairs is intuitive and based more on experience and past practice than on new approaches using learning outcomes mapping and assessment-based decision making.

In spite of these challenges, much progressive student affairs work is moving forward at Penn State. All practitioners who create or present educational programs have been invited to complete a comprehensive online learning module. The module teaches the concepts of Bloom's taxonomy (Bloom et al., 1956; Krathwohl, Bloom, and Masia, 1964), Penn

State co-curricular and first-year learning outcomes, and the skills needed to write and assess learning outcomes for educational workshops. With this new framework of outcomes in place, staff will be encouraged to apply appropriate assessment strategies to measure student achievement of those intended outcomes.

References

Bloom, B. S., Englehart, M. D., Furst, E. J, Hill, W., and Krathwohl, D. R. *Taxonomy of Educational Objectives: The Classification of Educational Goals. Handbook I: Cognitive Domain.* New York: Longmans Green, 1956.

Cleveland-Innes, M. F., and Emes, C. "Social and Academic Interaction in Higher Educational Contexts and the Effect on Deep Learning." *NASPA Journal*, 2005, *42*, 241–262.

Ignelzi, M. "Meaning-Making in the Learning and Teaching Process." In M. Baxter Magolda (ed.), *Teaching to Promote Intellectual and Personal Maturity: Incorporating Students' Worldviews and Identities into the Learning Process.* New Directions for Teaching and Learning, no. 82. San Francisco: Jossey-Bass, 2000.

Kegan, R. *In over Our Heads: The Mental Demands of Modern Life.* Cambridge. Mass.: Harvard University Press, 1994.

King, P. M. "Inviting College Students to Reflect on Their Collegiate Experiences." Paper presented at meeting of Conversation on the Liberal Arts Conference. Santa Barbara, Calif., 2007. Retrieved Oct. 7, 2007, from http://www.soe.umich.edu/liberalartstudy/downloads/Westmont2007.pdf.

Krathwohl, D. R., Bloom, B. S., and Masia, B. B. *Taxonomy of Educational Objectives: The Classification of Educational Goals. Handbook II: Affective Domain.* New York: Longmans Green, 1964.

Nash, R. *Liberating Scholarly Writing: The Power of Personal Narrative.* New York: Teachers College Press, 2004.

National Survey of Student Engagement. "Engaged Learning: Fostering Success for All Students." Annual Report 2006. Bloomington, Ind.: Indiana University, 2006. Retrieved Oct. 7, 2007, from http://nsse.iub.edu/NSSE_2006_Annual_Report/docs/NSSE_2006_Annual_Report.pdf.

Pascarella, E. T., and Terenzini, P. T. *How College Affects Students: A Third Decade of Research.* San Francisco: Jossey-Bass, 2005.

Penn State Division of Student Affairs. "Strategic Plan 2005–2008." 2005. Retrieved Oct. 7, 2007, from http://www.sa.psu.edu/stratplan/.

Reardon, R. C., Lumsden, J. A., and Meyer, K. E. "Developing an E-portfolio Program: Providing a Comprehensive Tool for Student Development, Reflection, and Integration." *NASPA Journal*, 2005, *42*, 368–380.

Upcraft, M. L., and Schuh, J. H. *Assessment in Student Affairs: A Guideline for Practitioners.* San Francisco: Jossey-Bass, 1996.

Volkwein, J. F. "On the Correspondence Between Objective and Self-reported Measures of Student Learning Outcomes" [online]. 2005. http://www.ed.psu.edu/cshe/abet/pdf/Self_Reported.pdf.

PHILIP J. BURLINGAME *serves as the associate vice president for student affairs at Pennsylvania State University.*

ANDREA L. DOWHOWER *has served as the director and senior analyst of student affairs research and assessment at Pennsylvania State University since 2004.*

NEW DIRECTIONS FOR STUDENT SERVICES • DOI: 10.1002/ss

11

This chapter provides a glimpse of student affairs assessment at California State University, Sacramento, including a specific example of assessment, tips to implementing assessment at your institution, and barriers encountered when implementing the process at California State University, Sacramento.

California State University, Sacramento

Lori E. Varlotta

Overview of Institutional Culture

California State University, Sacramento, commonly referred to as "Sacramento State," is a booming metropolitan university located on three hundred acres in the state capital of California. The university, the seventh largest in the California State University system, enrolls a multicultural student body of approximately twenty-nine thousand students. Though most students commute to class from their family home or nearby apartment, the university has an increasingly vibrant campus life with thousands of students staying on campus to study, eat, recreate, attend co-curricular programs, and work. Recently faculty and staff have begun to refer to the campus as a "resamuter" rather than a "commuter" one to connote the ongoing flurry of activity typically associated with a residential campus: students hanging out, setting up organizational booths, throwing balls on the quads, studying in small groups throughout academic buildings and the library, eating, socializing, attending events in the University Union, and living and learning in the residence halls. The campus offers high-quality undergraduate and master's programs. Additionally, it offers joint doctoral programs and one independent Ed.D. The campus has long been known for its commitment to both access and excellence. Sacramento State takes great pride in admitting and graduating students who have excelled in high school and community college, along with those who show promise in actualizing their potential.

NEW DIRECTIONS FOR STUDENT SERVICES, no. 127, Fall 2009 © Wiley Periodicals, Inc.
Published online in Wiley InterScience (www.interscience.wiley.com) • DOI: 10.1002/ss.332

Overview of Division of Student Affairs/Services

Shortly after she was appointed in spring 2005, the vice president of student affairs circulated a revised university mission to engage her own directors in a conversation about the division's mission. During initial management meetings that semester, the directors explained how their efforts to revitalize the division's mission had been delayed by vacancies at the top level of the division (the vice presidency and two associate vice presidential posts). Feeling a bit dejected by the false starts they had recently experienced, the directors were very open to the vice president's suggestion of having "new eyes" look at the mission statement. In consultation with her directors, the vice president formed an ad hoc task force of midlevel student affairs staff to begin anew the mission revision process.

This group of seven midlevel staff, dubbed the "mission committee," was excited by the charge to revisit and ultimately rewrite the division's mission statement and any corollary materials they deemed relevant. Within three months, the mission committee had collaborated with staff throughout the division to formulate drafts of the mission, vision, and values statements. The committee unveiled their work during a formal presentation delivered during a directors' meeting. After incorporating some of the feedback delivered at that meeting, the committee presented the finalized version of these statements (included here) at the December 2006 divisionwide meeting of all four-hundred-plus student affairs staff.

> *Vision:* As a vital component of a destination campus, Student Affairs will be a recognized leader in fostering student learning, growth, retention, and success at the university and beyond.

> *Mission:* The Division of Student Affairs at Sacramento State meets the diverse needs of our students by offering programs, services, and opportunities that empower students to reach their unique potential as learners, as contributing members of their communities, and as responsible leaders.

> *Core Values:*
> - *Integrity:* We pride ourselves on being honorable, trustworthy, and credible.
> - *Collaboration:* The interactive partnerships we forge with members of the division, the university, and the community enable us to create meaningful learning experiences for our students.
> - *Empowerment:* We help students develop the knowledge, skills, and attributes needed to shape their future.
> - *Respect for diversity:* We cultivate a culture of civility where the open exchange of ideas and respect for all people are paramount.
> - *Service to students:* We strive to deliver programs, policies, and services in a timely, respectful manner.

NEW DIRECTIONS FOR STUDENT SERVICES • DOI: 10.1002/ss

The mission, vision, and values statements are more than just words. Together, they clearly identify the division as learning-focused, with an emphasis on student success. At Sacramento State, student success ultimately relates to retention and graduation rates. However, as research shows, the chances for these outcomes are increased as students:

- Become more connected to other students, faculty, and staff—often via the programs and activities offered by Student Affairs (Astin, 1993; Tinto, 2002)
- Experience a sense of belonging or a feeling of being a part of the campus, again enhanced by many Student Affairs activities (Tinto, 1992)
- Access myriad academic and support programs that potentially increase their performance in the classroom (Nutt, 2003)

Cognizant of these student success predictors, staff within the division actively promote their programs in order to positively contribute to student success.

Meanwhile, new faculty are made aware of Student Affairs programs during the faculty orientation program offered every August. Continuing faculty receive updates on these programs during the regularly scheduled college and department meetings held throughout the year. The more well-informed faculty are, the more they refer their students to appropriate events, programs, services, and activities sponsored by the division.

Overview of the Assessment Process

Within Sacramento State's Division of Student Affairs, student learning is evaluated in a structured, ongoing process. This process is coordinated and facilitated by both the vice president for student affairs (VPSA) and colleagues from the Office of Institutional Research (OIR). The expertise of the OIR staff has significantly accelerated the assessment process with these colleagues serving as one-on-one assessment consultants to the student affairs directors. Working with OIR, the directors are expected to engage their entire staff in a six-step assessment process that confirms or challenges what students have learned by participating in their departments' programs and services. The six steps of the assessment process:

1. Writing (or revising) a departmental mission statement that is directly aligned with the missions of the university and the division
2. Formulating broad planning goals
3. Identifying measurable program objectives and student learning outcomes
4. Developing a methodology to measure those outcomes
5. Collecting and analyzing the data generated
6. Using the emergent information to make data-driven decisions that become part of an established culture of evidence

NEW DIRECTIONS FOR STUDENT SERVICES • DOI: 10.1002/ss

To organize their work at each step, directors use a specific reporting template. It ensures that the appropriate fields are completed and the information is collected and disseminated consistently throughout the division. The template used by the departments is posted at http://saweb.csus.edu/students/download/SA_Assessment_Plans2007.pdf.

Step one: Writing the departmental mission
Step two: Formulating planning goals
Step three: Identifying program objectives and student learning outcomes
Step four: Mapping out the methodology
Step five: Collecting and analyzing data
Step six: Using the emergent information to make data-driven decisions

Directors have little flexibility in deciding which of the aforementioned six steps they will complete. There is an explicit expectation—in fact, it is part of their annual performance review—that they will engage their staff in working through each and every step. Still, the directors do have significant latitude in determining how they will complete each step as goal formulation, outcome identification, instrument selection, and data analysis occur at the departmental level. In making these decisions, directors are encouraged to include staff input, student assistant, and student "user" input.

Example of Assessment and How Results Are Used

Three years ago, armed with national and campus data that correlated a student's participation in orientation with an immediate increase in satisfaction, a sense of belonging, and ultimately higher persistence and graduation rates, Sacramento State's Advising Center decided to significantly enhance its freshmen orientation program. To begin their work, staff formulated the program objective:

By summer 2006, transform the current three-fourths-day optional freshmen orientation into a day-and-a-half mandatory program with a strongly encouraged overnight experience. Ensure that the expanded program augments academic information sessions with a broader offering of co-curricular workshops. Offer an online alternative for confirmed circumstances that make it extremely difficult for a student to attend the on-campus program. Expect a 98 percent participation rate.

This objective is focused on improving the freshmen orientation program; therefore, it is a program objective rather than a student learning outcome.

This program objective is fairly well written. It specifically addresses a single program, staff can measure the increased breadth of sessions, it is aggressive yet attainable, it is results-oriented, and it identifies an actual timeline for making the change.

New Directions for Student Services • DOI: 10.1002/ss

The Advising Center achieved the objective by delivering a broad-based, one-and-a-half-day mandatory orientation program in summer 2006. Curious as to whether or not the expanded program was well received by students and their families, the orientation staff designed a program evaluation that primarily measured parent and student satisfaction. The overwhelmingly positive responses to questions such as these suggested that the new orientation program was largely successful:

- Overall, this freshmen orientation program met my needs as an incoming student (parent).
  o strongly disagree   o disagree   o not sure   o agree   o strongly agree
- I enjoyed meeting and getting to know the orientation peer counselors.
  o strongly disagree   o disagree   o not sure   o agree   o strongly agree
- I was pleased with the number and types of break-out sessions offered during the day-and-a-half program.
  o strongly disagree   o disagree   o not sure   o agree   o strongly agree

Responses to these and similar questions helped staff determine to what extent students were satisfied with their orientation experience. Responses also allowed the staff to gather information about timeliness, quality of mailings, and the breadth of the sessions. Because this type of information is critically important during early implementation of the program, it made sense for the Advising Center to have assessment focus on program improvement early on in program life. Once the program was developed and institutionalized, however, it made sense to augment "program improvement" questions with "student learning ones."

During the second year of the program (summer 2006), the orientation assessment instrument was rewritten in an attempt to augment satisfaction data with student learning outcomes. In their initial attempt, some of the staff proposed that four true-or-false questions be added to the program evaluation:

- T/F This orientation program helped me understand how the university is organized.
- T/F After participating in orientation, I can identify the three major components of the undergraduate degree.
- T/F I now know how to register for my classes and, if necessary, how to add and drop courses.
- T/F I know exactly how many and what types of credits I need in order to graduate.

When questions are posed in this way, however, the only outcomes that can be generated are *indirect* student learning outcomes. Responses to these questions reflect only a perceived (that is, self-reported) increase in knowledge or understanding rather than a demonstrated or confirmed increase in knowledge acquisition. To generate the *direct* student learning outcomes that most directors seek, staff must write questions that prompt students to reveal what they have actually learned. Compare the next questions with the ones immediately above.

> Sacramento State is organized into these five "divisions," each of which is led by a vice president:
> A. Academic Affairs, Student Affairs, Administration and Business, Advancement and Development, Human Resources
> B. Freshmen, sophomores, juniors, seniors, graduate students
> C. Arts and Sciences, Engineering, Business, Health and Human Services, Natural Sciences
>
> All undergraduate degrees at Sacramento State are made up of which of these components:
> A. Laboratory classes and lectures
> B. Classroom activities and extracurricular events
> C. A major, general education courses, and electives
>
> Which of these describe how you may drop a class (check all that apply):
> A. Stop attending the class
> B. Tell the professor—via email, voice mail, or in person—that you are no longer interested in the course
> C. Go online to your "My Sac State" account and complete an electronic drop form, submit the form, and check your account in twelve hours to see if the request is processed

Questions such as these were included on the summer 2006 pre- and posttests. Interestingly, the scores on the posttest were barely higher than those on the pretest during the first summer. Even more curious was the data that showed the vast majority of orientation attendees scoring exceedingly high on both the pretest and the posttest. After scrutinizing the data, the director spoke with the orientation leaders (upper class student employees). The student leaders admitted they had coached their attendees on both tests because they believed (erroneously, of course) that their continued employment as orientation leaders was contingent on "near-perfect" pretest and posttest responses.

Clearly, the assessment philosophy and strategy had not been communicated to the student leaders charged with administering the pretest and posttest. Moreover, mounting fear about job security had not been realized or addressed. Seeing this gap, the orientation staff brought the student leaders more fully into the assessment loop and gave them appropriate training. The next year's data (summer 2007) looked very different. As originally expected, posttest scores were much higher than pretest scores, suggesting that the orientation attendees retained much of the information presented.

NEW DIRECTIONS FOR STUDENT SERVICES • DOI: 10.1002/ss

Tips for Implementing the Process

Having just finished the second full year of this comprehensive assessment plan, Sacramento State offers tips to colleagues who are conceptualizing and implementing their own comprehensive, campuswide assessment program.

First, collaborate with colleagues both within and outside student affairs who have an expertise in outcome-based assessment. At Sacramento State, the partnership that Student Affairs forged with OIR was invaluable. If building a similar partnership with an OIR department on your campus is unlikely, consider other colleagues with whom you can partner. At many campuses, the student affairs staff hire faculty on an overload or course-reduction basis to work with them on assessment.

Second, ensure that all directors and their respective staff members have been adequately trained in assessment philosophies and strategies. Early in the process at Sacramento, the VPSA invited colleagues from the University of Central Florida to serve as short-term consultants. After the consultants' two-day workshop concluded, directors continued being trained through one-on-one meetings they had with OIR staff. As the aforementioned orientation example revealed, however, the training expectations were not carried out to the student level. Given that this is a problem, more student assistants are now receiving assessment training.

Third, consider implementing a highly structured process complete with templates. Such an approach is prescriptive, but most directors at Sacramento welcomed the structure, the easy-to-follow guidelines, and the templates.

Fourth, reward staff—using formal and informal mechanisms, everything from kudos for a job well done to notes to annual evaluations—for implementing their plan, even if student participants do not learn exactly what we had intended.

Finally, ensure that there is an infrastructure in place for sustaining the assessment program over the long run.

Overcoming Barriers to Assessing Student Learning and Development

When asked if there were any barriers that impeded their work in assessment, directors cited three. First, several directors explained that the less intensive training that entry- and midlevel staff received (compared to the directors themselves) reduced both the readiness and the confidence level of this critical group. Knowing that a comprehensive assessment program must engage staff throughout the division, additional training is now offered. Second, a few directors in the service-oriented departments (financial aid, admissions, student records) legitimately questioned whether a learning emphasis should take priority over a service emphasis. Understandably, they did not want to lessen their commitment to accurate, timely, and efficient service delivery. Balancing their service improvement focus with a learning focus took some time. (To review the learning outcomes formulated by these "service" departments, please see the Sacramento State assessment website, given earlier in this article.) Third, a few of the staff disclosed lingering fear that their assessment program was simply and solely a performance evaluation of them as individual professionals. Debunking this myth about the purpose of programmatic assessment is critical yet challenging. After all, there is some connection between successful programs and high-performing staff, but the connection is not always a linear or proportional one. Some of our best directors, particularly the creative ones who are willing to take a risk, have planned and implemented "program duds," which is completely acceptable, especially as part of a learning experience. Meanwhile, some of our less-established staff have routinely implemented highly successful programs they have inherited from their predecessors. The important thing in all of these cases is to create a culture where staff can freely and honestly raise their concerns, all of which should be addressed from a serious, problem-solving perspective.

References

Astin, A. W. *What Matters in College: Four Critical Years Revisited.* San Francisco: Jossey-Bass, 1993.

Nutt, C. L. "Academic Advising and Student Retention and Persistence." 2003. Retrieved Dec. 14, 2007, from http://www.nacada.ksu.edu/clearinghouse/advisingissues/retention.htm.

Tinto, V. *Leaving College: Rethinking the Causes and Cures of Student Attrition.* Chicago: University of Chicago Press, 1992.

Tinto, V. "Promoting Student Retention: Lesson Learned from the United States." 2002. Retrieved Dec. 14, 2007, from http.www.ean-edu.org/news/tinto-pratocon.pdf.

LORI E. VARLOTTA serves as vice president for student affairs at California State University, Sacramento.

NEW DIRECTIONS FOR STUDENT SERVICES • DOI: 10.1002/ss

12

This chapter provides a glimpse of student affairs assessment at Texas A&M University including a specific example of assessment, tips to implementing assessment at your institution, and barriers encountered when implementing the process at Texas A&M University.

Texas A&M University

Sandi Osters

Overview of Institutional Culture

Texas A&M University is a research extensive institution located in College Station. More than forty-five thousand students attend the university (about 20 percent are graduate or professional students). Academically, the university is known for its engineering, business, and agricultural and veterinary medicine programs, although there are more than 150 programs of study. The university operates under a "strong college model"; functions are decentralized and fairly independent. There are ten vice presidents in the president's cabinet. The Division of Student Affairs, with more than six hundred full-time staff, reports through the executive vice president and provost. The division comprises sixteen departments. Beyond academics, the university is known for high student involvement and spirit among the students. There are more than eight hundred recognized student organizations, classified into three broad categories according to the complexity of the groups. They range from academic and professional to religious, sports-related, spirit and traditions, and performance and visual arts groups. There are fifty-six chapters included in a relatively new Greek system, and the Student Government Association coordinates at least fourteen programming committees. The majority of Texas A&M students participate in service and volunteerism through their organizations. Recent assessments reveal that about 70–80 percent of the students are active in at least one student organization at any time. The high-level student involvement frustrates some

NEW DIRECTIONS FOR STUDENT SERVICES, no. 127, Fall 2009 © Wiley Periodicals, Inc.
Published online in Wiley InterScience (www.interscience.wiley.com) • DOI: 10.1002/ss.333

faculty, but others see it as an opportunity for students to apply what they have learned in the classroom.

Overview of the Division of Student Affairs

The Division of Student Affairs' mission is "to facilitate student learning both in and out of the classroom by providing continuously improving, high-quality services and developmental opportunities while fostering an inclusive campus community in support of the educational mission of Texas A&M University." The core values are caring, diversity, respect, integrity, excellence, and service. The division's main purpose is to support the pre-eminent academic mission of the institution.

The Student Affairs departments themselves vary in the amount and nature of contact with faculty. The differences among cooperation, collaboration, and integration are not clearly defined when it comes to reporting faculty involvement in the Division of Student Affairs. Many use the terms interchangeably when in reality they reflect very different relationships. The staff in the Division of Student Affairs cooperate well, collaborate at every opportunity, and are working toward true integration of academic and co-curricular experience as one seamless learning experience. The road is long and the journey in its beginning stages. Although the university and the division do not have a comprehensive list of learning outcomes, the Student Leader Learning Outcomes (SLLO) project hopes to fill a void in that area.

Overview of the Assessment Process

In the summer of 2005, during a learning outcomes training workshop for student leaders and organization advisors, the observation arose that there were probably similar skill sets that students should develop regardless of the organizational context. As a result, the Department of Student Life Studies brought together more than thirty student affairs professionals from throughout the division to identify a set of shared learning outcomes for students who serve in positions of leadership across the university and determine methods in which to evaluate progress. This similarity in developmental goals and desired outcomes has generated synergy and enthusiasm throughout the life of the project.

The purpose of the SLLO is to promote consistent methods and tools for staff to use with student leaders in student organizations, programs, or activities to help in assessment and documentation of enhanced learning in relation to their leadership experiences. The particular goals of the program are:

- Develop learning outcomes for student leadership experiences in the co-curricular for use by advisors across the Division of Student Affairs and in academic departments.

NEW DIRECTIONS FOR STUDENT SERVICES • DOI: 10.1002/ss

- Develop assessment tools and methods for student learning outcomes.
- Create the infrastructure to market to and train staff in use of outcomes, assessment methods, and results.
- Prepare student leaders to be peer developers,
- Produce evidence of the value added by students' participation in co-curricular leadership experiences for use in accreditation, recruitment, fund raising, and development.
- Work collaboratively with colleges, the Career Center, and individual student leaders for documentation of student leadership learning through use of e-portfolios.
- Assist students with integration of learning between curricular and co-curricular experiences.

At the same time the goals were being created, the actual "work" of the group continued. The initial brainstorming event had produced nearly forty outcomes that were eventually categorized into themes. The SLLO committee prioritized skills and chose five of the highest for development as student leader learning outcomes. These five (which quickly became seven) were (1) project management, (2) communication (verbal, written, and interpersonal), (3) groups and teams, (4) critical thinking, and (5) diversity. Subcommittees were created to develop the outcomes, select a model or literature base, and design assessment rubrics and tools for the five selected skills.

It is important to note that theoretical frames of reference were selected for each in order to ground the goals in literature and research. Some of the outcomes are now based on a single theory or model, while others are a combination of several congruent theories and models. Subcommittees continued to refine their work, and encouragement came from the whole committee to test the rubrics with student leaders and student organizations. Various efforts have been initiated to pilot-test the usability of the tools, which were created around these first five outcomes. Findings from these early pilot tests were shared with the larger group; they informed further development of existing and future learning outcomes and assessment tools.

As the project continued, new subcommittees developed for marketing SLLO to students and other advisors; for training advisors and developing additional tools to support each skill and rubric; for meta assessment of the project on the basis of program outcomes, process outcomes, and the aggregate outcomes from the many students and advisors who will use these rubrics; and for infusing the concepts of reflection and seamless integration of learning into all of the rubrics. This has been and continues to be a work in progress. The process has been a very inductive and fluid one. Members of the committee have the comfort of moving in and out of the process as their time permits.

Staff advisors and student leaders are responsible for determining how the assessment will be used within the organization and at what point

NEW DIRECTIONS FOR STUDENT SERVICES • DOI: 10.1002/ss

students will be evaluated. For the most part, assessment rubrics are designed to be used as self-assessment tools and tools for a peer or staff evaluator. There are many models of student organizations and their leadership and advising structure. Thus there will be very different approaches to how the rubrics are used. One of the strengths of the SLLO is that the skills and assessment rubrics can function within the context of a particular organization and their approach to student leadership, while still being a comprehensive approach to assess an identified skill or outcome. Ultimately, however, a professional staff member will need to substantiate the extent to which the skill has been achieved for confirmation in an electronic portfolio at the Career Center or in a letter of reference.

SLLO is in its infancy. Some of the rubric development was assisted by faculty within discipline specific areas such as communications. Faculty members who are aware of the project through contact with Student Affairs administrators, or through programs attended by both, have started to ask for copies of the rubrics for use in the classroom. As the SLLO project moves beyond the group of approximately three dozen staff members who are on the committee, it will be brought to all Student Affairs advisors and eventually to all university faculty and staff who advise student organizations. The SLLO committee met specifically with the faculty member who oversees the College of Business learning outcomes project. The SLLO outcomes have been tracked to the college's learning outcomes, and students' work in the co-curricular may be used to satisfy requirements for curricular outcomes.

Example of Assessment and How Results Are Used

To create assessment tools for the student leader learning outcomes, small groups of staff members followed a series of common steps. Using the list generated during the brainstorming session, staff members volunteered to develop specific topics such as diversity, communication, and project management. Once the group logistics were determined, members spent time defining what student leaders needed to accomplish within that skill set. This included breaking the skill sets into smaller, more manageable components and creating process goals. For instance, the communication group recognized the importance of different types of communication and created three components (written, oral, and interpersonal) so they could focus on specific outcomes in each type.

Once the first seven rubrics were approved by the SLLO committee, many of the advisors developed a "just do it" philosophy and hit the ground running with their student leaders. One example is from the Memorial Student Center (MSC), the student union on campus. The first student organization to use a set of rubrics was a freshman leadership group committed to student development through service. This committee, MSC Freshmen in Service and Hosting (FISH), comprised sixty-six general committee members (freshmen), twelve assistant directors (sophomores), four executive directors (juniors), one vice chair (junior), and one chair (junior). FISH is responsible for producing campuswide programs throughout the year ranging from fundraisers to lectures to a conference for high school students. Each executive director is in charge of one area of concentration, such as financial development, and has two or three assistant directors (ADs) who report directly to him or her. Each area then plans, organizes, and facilitates programs according to its specific area of concentration. For example, financial development plans and executes all fundraisers for the committee.

Because of the nature of the organization and the duties of the student leaders, the project management rubric was selected to help analyze growth on forming goals, setting tasks, delegating, budgeting, risk management, and assessment. After completion of each student leader's initial project in the fall, he or she completed a self-evaluation with the project management assessment tool. The chair, vice chair, and advisor also evaluated each student on strengths and weaknesses within project management. Individual meetings were set up with students to review areas in which the student excelled, as well as areas that needed improvement. Subsequent evaluations were completed in February and April to track students' growth within the model.

The students' acceptance of this model was overwhelmingly positive, and their leadership and organizational skills have improved dramatically. Five of these students have been offered higher leadership positions within the student union council; they attribute their growth to using this assessment tool. In a focus group discussion regarding use of the rubric, the students overwhelmingly agreed that using it to identify their strengths and growth areas had been a very beneficial process for them as organization leaders as well as in their academic pursuits. They could clearly articulate their learning, ability to apply skills in other contexts, and skill in explaining their growth to others.

Tips for Implementing the Process

One of the most accessible and advantageous ways of learning about new programs and services is to learn from the experiences of others. Institutions are often able to gather and discern valuable design and implementation strategies based on the challenges and successes of the originating institution's experiences. The development of Student Leader Learning Outcomes will be no exception to this manner of program development. Although the process of developing Student Leader Learning Outcomes has been exceptionally successful at Texas A&M, each institution that is interested in developing a similar system for evaluating student learning will need to design and develop its own unique system congruent with the institutional mission, priorities, and processes.

From the experiences Texas A&M has shared in this process, we believe there are several key facets to consider as best practices, and we encourage institutions to replicate or adopt them. Our lessons could fill pages of text, but for the purposes of this case study we include a few representative examples of valuable lessons that we have learned along the way.

First of all, institutions should include individuals from a broad representation of staff and advisors at the institution to create as much buy-in and excitement as possible. Some staff members at Texas A&M were skeptical about measuring out-of-class learning with tools such as rubrics, but there were a group of early adopters who shared contagious enthusiasm about the prospects of this process. Our initial brainstorming session, which generated a list of more than thirty outcomes, included staff members from across the Division of Student Affairs and had multiple levels of leadership represented, ranging from graduate assistants to department heads and an assistant vice president of student affairs.

The people involved in the process will be a key to your success; we also recommend that you consider the culture of leadership development on your campus (for example, models, theories, and definitions of leadership that inform your practice). Our experience has been that various contexts for leadership development exist on our campus and determining a shared definition of leadership would have created a barrier to our progress rather than helping us move forward with this initiative. We have been successful in defining outcomes that fit and support multiple contexts for leadership development and are congruent with a variety of leadership practices. Various models of leadership development are represented in our working group—including business, military, and public service models—as well as philosophy statements that are unique to some of the departments within our division.

Our initial list of outcomes included a comprehensive view of desired outcomes for student leaders. We encourage campuses to think as broadly as possible in the initial brainstorming of desired outcomes and then select the most important outcomes for which you will build measurement tools and strategies. This being said, remember that each area represented within your team will be passionate about its own types of outcomes, so make your initial efforts at developing rubrics and measurement tools broad enough to capitalize on these diverse interests.

Perhaps one of our greatest achievements in this process was our decision to ground the definition of each outcome and associated assessment measure in theory or a relevant model. Faculty members who have become aware of our work have applauded our efforts to ground outcomes and rubrics in at least one theory or model. We also feel this theoretical foundation will be important for the training component of our work with advisors and student leaders, because they can gain a sense of the conceptual background behind the desired outcome and behaviors for student leaders.

In summary, from the work that has been created and implemented at Texas A&M University, we would strongly encourage institutions to incorporate three aspects of our project: (1) collaboration, (2) rubric development, and (3) training. The collaboration that initiated the project and continues through today and has allowed creation of a stronger project as staff from multiple offices provide feedback, ideas, and suggestions on every aspect. The feedback received has been from areas across the Division of Student Affairs and has allowed us to create a project that is full of perspectives, recognition of our need to work with different populations, and the ability to create a stronger product thanks to the diversity and experience of those involved in its creation.

Overcoming Barriers to Assessing Student Learning and Development

From the outset of this project, staff members involved in its creation and eventual implementation recognized the depth and breadth of what was being tackled. One specific barrier that might have sidelined the project was the initial goal: creation of a campuswide student leader learning outcome process. The very word *campuswide* at a larger institution has the potential to sideline a project before it can even get off the ground. Barriers could have been created by arguments among the team over word definitions, project goals, and implementation timelines. These obstacles were avoided by this team's desire to create something truly unique and transformative. The bringing together of colleagues who rarely work together and many who had never met was not a barrier, but instead a strength. The people involved work with students daily, have at least some authority over their work environment, and do not face the same political limitations that department directors do. The team had many advantages in the skill sets the members possessed, the facilitation skills on the part of the project organizers, and the group's overwhelming desire to create something great not only for our students but also for ourselves.

In addition, time clearly became a potential barrier from the start of the project. Staff were busy with their own work, many departments had vacancies (which required staff to do more work), and this project had not been established as a division priority. To accommodate these issues, staff were reminded that they were welcome to participate as they could; for some staff this meant taking time off from the group when their job duties were particularly demanding (for example, orientation staff in the spring are busy preparing for summer events, but residence hall staff may have more flexibility then). Having a large group is a definite advantage in this regard. Staff were also encouraged to join a subcommittee that developed learning outcomes and an assessment method for a particular skill area. Student Life Studies worked with the division directors and the vice president's office to promote this project, show how it supported the mission of the division and the university, and provide feedback along the way about implementation of the project. Regardless of the challenges, this unique group of colleagues

New Directions for Student Services • DOI: 10.1002/ss

have kept their eye on the prize: providing evidence of the value added by students' participation in co-curricular leadership experiences and ensuring continuous improvement in the content and its process.

SANDI OSTERS is the director of student life studies at Texas A&M University.

NEW DIRECTIONS FOR STUDENT SERVICES • DOI: 10.1002/ss

13

This chapter provides a glimpse of student affairs assessment at Widener University including a specific example of assessment, tips to implementing assessment at your institution, and barriers encountered when implementing the process at Widener University.

Widener University

Brigitte Valesey, Jo Allen

Overview of Institutional Culture

Founded in 1821, Widener University is a two-state (Pennsylvania and Delaware), four-campus, eight-college private institution serving approximately sixty-seven hundred students. Widener's history is unique in many aspects. Originally founded as a Quaker school for boys before transforming into a military college that later transformed yet again into the current coed, nonmilitary university, Widener most recently underwent a substantial visioning process that drew input from faculty, staff, students, community leaders, alumni, board members, employers, and partners from every community we touch. The process resulted in a new mission, vision, and strategic plan that center on the singular distinctive commonality that runs throughout Widener's history: its commitment to service and leadership. The university has recently received extraordinary national attention, largely from the integration of its planning, assessment, reaccreditation, and campaign planning processes, as well as for its mission-focused work with civic engagement as the best means for promoting active scholarship and preparing students for their lives as citizens of character. Meeting the imperatives of our mission and furthering our national reputation has led to substantial work in revising and reassessing our curriculum through general education offerings, first-year experience programming, and leadership programming, as well as service learning, community-based research, internships and cooperative education, and other forms of experiential learning.

NEW DIRECTIONS FOR STUDENT SERVICES, no. 127, Fall 2009 © Wiley Periodicals, Inc.
Published online in Wiley InterScience (www.interscience.wiley.com) • DOI: 10.1002/ss.334

Overview of Division of Student Affairs

Following arrival of the new senior vice president and provost in 2004 and subsequent reorganization of vice presidential responsibilities, Student Affairs is now led by a dean of students who reports to the senior vice president and provost. Historically, co-curricular programming and other aspects of Student Affairs have been a bit marginalized by a large segment of the campus population, which may have been operating on a "need to know" basis in regard to student life issues. As a result, it is likely that student affairs and its work were either invisible to the community when things were running well or, alternatively, viewed as "in crisis" when things were running poorly. As a result of recent restructuring, however, the potential for Student Affairs to enjoy more daily recognition is substantial, allowing it to move into the mainstream of the university's vision for promoting student development and learning. This movement and potential are readily evidenced by its staff's inclusion in strategic planning, and more recently as members on the two key committees (design and then implementation) involved with assessment of student learning.

Student Affairs staff engaged in a strategic planning process over a six-month period, culminating in a strategic plan that articulates a vision, mission, and set of strategic objectives aligned with the university's strategic plan and priorities. The mission guides the work of Student Affairs:

> Mission: Student Affairs is dedicated to the holistic development of our students so that they accomplish their educational goals and become responsible, productive and civically engaged citizens in a global community. We actively collaborate within and beyond the university to achieve Widener's strategic mission. We integrate services and programs to promote student leadership and character development. We foster a community that contributes to students' intellectual, spiritual, social, cultural, moral and emotional growth [Widener University, 2006].

From the School of Law's focus on *pro bono* and clinical work addressing veterans' rights, domestic violence victims' rights, and environmental transgressions to the Division of Social Work's efforts to establish a Spanish-speaking living and learning community that focuses on the social work needs of the Hispanic community in Chester, Pennsylvania, Widener proudly continues to build strong curricular and co-curricular experiences for students interested in understanding their roles and responsibilities as educated citizens with the capacity for making change in a democracy. As a result of their participation in student affairs programming, students are expected to develop co-curricular perspectives on civic engagement and broaden their roles and responsibilities as citizens of character in global societies. Our institutional learning outcomes encourage powerful possibilities for co-curricular integration with curricular offerings:

NEW DIRECTIONS FOR STUDENT SERVICES • DOI: 10.1002/ss

- Students will demonstrate the knowledge, skills, and scholarship that are appropriate for their field of study.
- Students will be able to think critically and communicate effectively.
- Students will demonstrate attributes associated with professional and civic leadership.
- Students will demonstrate characteristics of responsible citizenship.

Overview of the Assessment Process

As a campus unit, Student Affairs has been engaged in formal university-wide conversations about assessment of student learning since fall 2004. Assessment culture building with the unit was recognized as a crucial step in advancing assessment within the unit, because of the number of new staff persons hired in a relatively short time. The associate dean for student programs was designated as the person responsible for coordinating and communicating assessment activities. In consultation with the assistant provost for student learning assessment, the associate dean coordinated activities aimed at engaging staff, gathering input and assessment data, and providing feedback.

Prior to planning for assessment of student learning, staff meetings focused on developing a strategic plan for the unit. The strategic plan articulated the mission, vision, and goals for Student Affairs and identified strategic initiatives to be accomplished by each program. The strategic planning activities developed common direction and vision for the staff and established clear priorities for the next several years. Although the staff understood the strategic planning process and shared a common vision, they were less clear about how strategic planning differed from planning for student learning assessment. Retreat activities allowed comparison of the two types of plans and their purposes. Through discussion, staff identified distinctions and intersections of the plans as well as ways to integrate planning activities and processes. Both strategic and assessment plans and processes were deemed essential by staff to determine the successes of programming experiences and quality of services. Staff recognized the complementary nature of strategic plans and assessment plans.

The staff participated in two retreats designed to address assessment from the student affairs context and to frame unit-level learning objectives. During the first retreat, Assessment Journey: From Student Satisfaction to Student Learning and Development, the staff affirmed assumptions concerning assessment:

- Student Affairs programming and activities contribute to what students learn about themselves and the world around them.
- Gathering information and data helps us understand how well our programs are working and what they contribute to student growth and development (Bresciani, Zelna, and Anderson, 2004).

- We are already engaging in some assessment activities.
- Assessment can be done with existing resources.
- Outcomes for assessment should be meaningful, measurable, and manageable (Bresciani, Zelna, and Anderson, 2004).

Assessment of student learning, for Student Affairs, was presented and carried out as a collaborative and iterative process, as shown in Figure 13.1. Staff recognized the value of established, clear, and concise learning objectives to guide activities and assessment. Programming and related activities were framed as opportunities for student learning and growth, designed to contribute to attainment of the learning objectives. Assessment activities and measures that would yield measures of student learning and development were identified. Reporting mechanisms and timelines were established to permit regular reporting out to the full staff and other constituencies.

In addressing the purposes for assessing learning from the Student Affairs perspective, participants agreed that learning should be assessed in order to improve programming quality, to maximize student growth and development; inform planning and decision making; and create a culture of continuous improvement. Assessment, from an historical perspective, needed to move beyond student satisfaction measures to more closely address learning *priorities* for Student Affairs and for the university.

Development of learning objectives—broad statements describing student affairs' expectations for what students should know, do, and become— grew out of staff discussions related to these key questions: What are high-priority expectations for student learning, from various program perspectives? How do they relate to the student affairs mission and goals? How do they embrace what student affairs programs desire to accomplish? The staff brainstormed an initial list of twenty learning expectations. The six learning objectives given here evolved out of further discussion.

Figure 13.1. Student Affairs Assessment Process

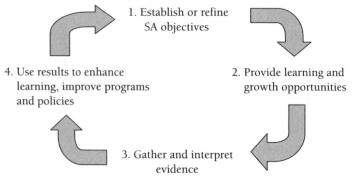

1. Establish or refine SA objectives

2. Provide learning and growth opportunities

3. Gather and interpret evidence

4. Use results to enhance learning, improve programs and policies

Adapted from: *Student Learning Assessment, Options and Resources*, Middle States Commission on Higher Education, 2003.

1. Clarify personal values and demonstrate ethical behavior.
2. Promote responsible citizenship.
3. Develop a sense of autonomy, maturity, and personal responsibility.
4. Enhance appreciation of human differences.
5. Establish and maintain a healthy and balanced lifestyle—physically, mentally, spiritually, and emotionally.
6. Demonstrate leadership knowledge and skill.

These learning objectives reflect the vision, mission, and values of the unit and are aligned with the mission and goals of the institution as described in the strategic plan. As of the first retreat, the staff had recently completed the student affairs strategic plan, which was reflected in the language of the objectives and close alignment with strategic initiatives.

Recognizing that Student Affairs learning experiences contribute to attainment of general education goals, the staff mapped the general education goals with the six new learning objectives. The experience was informative to staff, because there was significant alignment. The process of mapping general education goals to Student Affairs learning objectives affirmed the significant contributions of student affairs experiences in the learning processes and results. A similar process was used by the staff to map the learning objectives to the institutional learning objectives.

Using information from the second retreat, staff from each program developed a set of learning outcomes. This process reflected the range of expectations, from enhancing diversity to individual wellness to community engagement. After the retreat, each set of program outcomes was aligned with the Student Affairs learning objectives to allow a holistic review of the contributions to learning in various programs as aligned with the overarching objectives. Aligning objectives and outcomes across programs constituted the basis for staff discussion concerning programmatic strengths as well as possible learning and assessment gaps.

The full-day staff retreats made dedicated time available for staff to engage in a collaborative assessment planning effort. Significant progress and understanding resulted from this focused effort. Staff feedback from the retreats reflected the value of this planning activity. Staff within each program were responsible for developing a plan for student learning assessment. This meant documenting learning outcomes, assessment methods, multiple measures, timelines, and persons responsible for collecting the data and information as well as reporting out. Staff engaged in a collaborative process for articulating what students are expected to learn, in the form of desired knowledge, target performances, and attitudes as well as value-added benefits. Through full staff and program-level discussions, staff shifted focus from strictly program outcomes to what students will achieve as a result of participating in Student Affairs programs.

In identifying appropriate assessment tools and measures, staff engaged in discussion regarding use of institutional research data. Staff were

NEW DIRECTIONS FOR STUDENT SERVICES • DOI: 10.1002/ss

encouraged to review pertinent institutional data and use data results and analyses to inform assessment activities. Preliminary discussion concerning gathering of longitudinal data was part of the assessment conversation. Consultations with the assistant provost for assessment resulted in these guidelines:

- Look for multiple sources of data to use as a baseline, for comparison purposes, to establish assessment criteria.
- Use institutional data to inform learning and assessment decisions.
- Consider pooling data from other units on campus, such as Campus Safety data reports, school or college orientation surveys, and information and instructional technology data.
- Establish target dates for reviewing and reporting program and unit-level data.
- Consider combining some survey and focus group activities from across programs.

Example of Assessment and How Results Are Used

As one unit within Student Affairs, Student Life coordinates a range of programming and student activities, from student clubs and organizations to Family Day and Weekend programs and orientation programs. Student Life articulates these learning outcomes:

- Students will learn about community service opportunities and the benefits of participating.
- Students who attend the orientation program will be able to better transition into Widener as new students.
- Fraternities and sororities will take responsibility for actions.
- Student organization members will demonstrate leadership skills by independently coordinating events, organizing meetings, recruiting members, and presenting programs.
- Student Life programming supports freshmen transitions, involvement in campus and volunteer organizations, and student leadership opportunities.

Articulated in the Student Life program assessment plan is the use of varied measures to assess what students and other participants learn from various experiences, and their level of satisfaction. Strategies for assessing outcomes include surveys, focus groups, event participation numbers, judicial records and reports, and formal evaluations of student organizations. Several assessment measures are used to collect information concerning freshman orientation.

The Freshman Orientation Program marks a key transition for first-year students entering the university. Historically, the program consisted of several one-and-a-half-day summer sessions and a weeklong fall program beginning when freshmen arrive after Labor Day. In the summer orientation sessions, incoming freshmen and their parents participated in various campus sessions designed to acquaint students with the expectations and resources associated with college learning and living. Activities during the day focused on academic expectations, placement, and campus orientation while evening sessions focused on social transitions. During the summer session, students took placement tests and completed writing samples as part of the orientation activities. In the fall program, students had both required and optional activities interspersed over the week. Events were scheduled on the fall orientation days.

Assessments in the form of satisfaction surveys and focus groups conducted in fall 2004 provided student feedback concerning the programs. In spring 2005, an orientation advisory committee was established to reexamine the orientation program in response to assessment feedback. The advisory committee reviewed best practices at peer and benchmarked institutions, attended conferences to gather information, and reviewed the efficacy of current orientation practices. Coincident to this development was the restructuring of student services related to enrollment and financial aid; the Enrollment Management Services (EMS) unit was created to bring consistency and efficiency to these operations. Creation of the EMS unit yielded greater consistency in expectations and orientation program objectives. The advisory committee examined ways to be more responsive to students and to implement a highly student-centered approach to orientation. The fall orientation timeline was considered particularly problematic and conflicted with athletic schedules, arrival of returning students, and other student programs.

New orientation programs recommended by the advisory committee were approved in spring 2006 and implemented in the 2006–07 academic year. Summer programs were reduced to a single day of activity, with the focus on enrollment and financial aid activities, placement testing, and campus orientation. Student and parents participated in parallel information sessions. For the fall 2006 program, orientation shifted to a three-day, more formal, and mandatory program. Program objectives placed greater emphasis on the high school to university transition, on community building and bonding activities, and on orientation as an academic requirement. Evening programs focused on topics including maximizing the college experience and alcohol education. Increased faculty and staff collaboration in first-year workshops and evening presentations contributed to the meeting program's objectives.

The orientation assessment survey was redesigned to be more student- and learning-centered. Survey items peripheral to the experience and not aligned with student life outcomes were deleted. After the new orientation program was implemented, summer and fall orientation satisfaction surveys were administered, and the results were compiled and reviewed. Survey results indicated that most students agreed the orientation program, including academics, student responsibilities, and social involvement, prepared them for addressing expectations related to college life. Students responded that the orientation program was most helpful in meeting other people, fostering an adjustment period, and teaching them how to make the most of the college experience (Manning and Kator, 2006). Student focus groups were also held to collect information concerning the orientation experience. Student responses from focus group sessions and summer surveys expressed the need for incoming freshmen to have more socialization time in the form of such activities as "ice breakers," student-to-student Q & A sessions, and opportunities to talk with current students.

The assessment results for the summer and fall 2006 orientation program were reviewed by student affairs staff, the orientation advisory committee, and other stakeholders. Analyses of results yielded several recommendations for subsequent orientations:

• Build more topics of diversity education into the program.
• Provide better inclusion and participation of commuter students.
• Provide more direct contact with faculty before classes begin.
• Offer an online alcohol education program.
• Bring in more nationally recognized presenters for evening sessions.
• Change venues (facilities) to better target the audience [Manning and Kator, 2006].

These assessment results have driven formal discussion about phasing in changes to the orientation program and customized orientation sessions for commuters and other student groups. Additionally, the conversations and data have demonstrated where additional resources for personnel and programming might be best used.

Tips for Implementing the Process

Assessment of student learning in Student Affairs at Widener University is evolving into a systematic and ongoing process. The assessment process reflects the culture for both continuous process improvement and assessment that has evolved at Widener and constitutes a model for other co-curricular programs. Successful assessment practices reflect staff involvement throughout the assessment planning and implementation process, coordination of activities and reporting by a designated staff person, and staff commitment to using results to make improvements. Accountability is further ensured by inclusion of regular assessment updates in quarterly performance reviews of the dean of students, and in the annual goal setting and subsequent review of staff performances.

Successful implementation of assessment can be attributed to several factors. Student Affairs staff were collectively responsible for development of the assessment processes and decision making, assuming ownership for assessment. A staff person in charge of assessment ensured coordination of assessment activities and follow-through. Additionally, staff communicate regularly about assessment activities and results in staff meetings. The linkages between the university and unit strategic plans and assessment activities contribute to the value of assessment.

References

Bresciani, M. J., Zelna, C. L., and Anderson, J. A. *Assessing Student Learning and Development: A Handbook for Practitioners.* Washington D.C.: National Association of Student Personnel Administrators, 2004.

Manning, K., and Kator, T. "Briefing on Fall Orientation." Presentation to senior leadership team, Widener University, Chester, Penn. 2006.

Middle States Commission on Higher Education. *Student Learning Assessment, Options and Resources.* Philadelphia: Middle States Commission on Higher Education, 2003.

Widener University. *Student Affairs Strategic Plan.* Chester, Penn.: Widener University, 2006.

BRIGITTE VALESEY is the assistant provost for teaching, learning, and assessment at Widener University.

JO ALLEN is the senior vice president and provost at Widener University.

INDEX